The Benn Heresy

Alan Freeman

The Benn Heresy

Pluto Press

First published by Pluto Press Limited
Unit 10 Spencer Court, 7 Chalcot Road, London NW1 8LH

British Library Cataloguing in Publication Data:
Freeman, Alan
The Benn heresy.
1. Benn, Tony 2. Political science—Great Britain—History 3. Socialism in Great Britain
I. Title
320.5′315′0924 JC257.B/
ISBN 0-86104-363-4

Cover designed by Clive Challis
Cover photograph by N. Sagansky, Negative Press

Photoset by Photobooks (Bristol) Limited,
Barton Manor, St Philips, Bristol BS2 ORN
Printed in Great Britain by St Edmundsbury Press Limited,
Bury St Edmunds, Suffolk IP33 3TU

Contents

Dedicated to the memory of Neil Williamson

Acknowledgements

Amongst many whose work I have drawn on, special mention must be made of Robert Jenkins' valuable biography, of the collections of speeches and writings edited by Joan Bodington and Chris Mullin, and the very useful and painstaking enquiry into the effects of Labour's industrial policy by all who took part in the *Workers' Enquiry* into the 1974-79 Labour government.

Thanks for the help or advice of Stephen Potter, John Harrison, Chris Freeman, Dave Bailey, Jon Lansman, Mike Tichelar, and all my co-journalists at *Socialist Challenge*; for the inspiration and influence of my comrades of the international socialist movement, particularly the Fourth International; and to the workers of Meriden, Kirkby Manufacturing Enterprises, Maclaren Controls, Laurence Scott Electromotors; to activists of the Campaign for Labour Party Democracy, the Labour Co-ordinating Committee, the Rank and File Mobilising Committee and many more who in fighting for their rights have made Bennism a movement as well as an idea.

Last but not least, my thanks to Tony Benn for the time he has spent discussing his ideas with me and commenting on various drafts of the manuscript. I can think of few other politicians who would spend so much time and care assisting their critics.

Prologue

> I pondered all these things, and how men fight and lose the battle, and the thing they fought for comes about in spite of their defeat, and when it comes turns out not to be what they meant. And other men have to fight for what they meant under another name.
>
> William Morris *News from Nowhere*

On 3 October 1957, delegates to Labour's annual conference sat in packed ranks in Brighton's Corn Exchange to debate the British H-bomb. Norwood resolution 24 called for the unilateral renunciation of the testing, manufacture or use of nuclear weapons in any form. For the motion: the Labour left. Against: The Labour right.

The hall quietened as a giant rose to speak. Nye Bevan, hero of the left, symbol of the moral, political and physical struggle of British working people, was about to announce the end of an era.

'When Bevan sat down', wrote an MP later, 'I had to get up and go away. I couldn't stand any more . . . I had been present at a murder – the murder of the enthusiasm that built the Labour movement'.

Bevan had done the unthinkable. He had spelled out to his thunderstruck supporters why they should oppose the Norwood resolution.

Bevan died in 1960, but Bevanism – the movement which dominated Labour's left-right battle throughout the fifties, and which embodied all the hopes and aspirations of the forties – died that night.

The years that followed saw the formal triumph of the Bevan team. His former colleagues rose to power one by one: Harold Wilson, who had resigned with him from Attlee's 1950 Cabinet, became Labour's longest-serving prime minister in history; Michael Foot, who led the unilateralists to their short-lived victory at

Labour's 1960 conference in Scarborough, replaced Wilson's disgraced successor Callaghan as party leader in 1980. But the events of the sixties and seventies tested Bevan's inheritance to its limits – and found it wanting. The Bevanite team presided, in two successive governments and two successive decades, over the dismantling of almost everything Bevan had stood for.

A gap opened up on the left of the Labour Party. Today it is being filled by supporters of a new symbol of Labour's socialist ideals: Anthony Neill Wedgwood Benn. The aim of this book is to explain how this came about.

Benn's background was very different from Bevan's. He was born on 3 April 1925, almost within earshot of Westminster. His father, William Wedgwood Benn, had been a radical Liberal MP since 1906. In 1928 William entered the Commons as a Labour MP. In 1941 he was made Viscount Stansgate. The title passed to his son on his death in 1960.

Benn's mother, Margaret Eadie Holmes, was the granddaughter of a Perthshire engineer who, after founding the firm of Eadie Brothers, became provost of Paisley. Her father, Daniel Turner Holmes, served as Liberal MP for Govan from 1910 to 1918.

Benn's family was radical and dissenting. In the 1892 election his grandfather John Benn campaigned as 'MP for the back streets' with Irish Home Rule as a campaign theme. His father broke with Lloyd George over his postwar coalition policies and on the Home Rule issue. Both were nurtured in the old Liberal principles of democratic rights, government in the interests of the people, and opposition to the use of force as an instrument of foreign policy. His mother became a Congregationalist at the age of fifty-one, having studied theology at King's College, London. Scottish Presbyterianism and fundamentalism, with their fierce insistence on moral principle and rejection of ecclesiastical authority, were strong traditions in her family.

His radical commitment was nurtured and deepened by a political partnership with his wife, Caroline Middleton de Camp, whom he met in 1948 and married the year after. An American of dissenting Huguenot stock, Caroline became a campaigner for the socialist movement for educational reform in Britain. Later on, as the distance between Benn and his colleagues in the Labour leadership began to grow, Caroline's experience and influence were to become a major factor in shaping his emerging political philosophy.

But his was neither a working class, nor a socialist background. His uncle, Ernest Benn, was a fierce defender of free enterprise, also in the old Liberal tradition. His book *Confessions of a Capitalist* expounded the ideas he used to denounce Churchill for paving the way to socialism. It was almost as if the Benn family had set itself the task of reproducing within its ranks the historic split within Liberalism which led to its replacement by the Labour Party.

Benn's family was not aristocratic and his father's peerage owed more to wartime realpolitik than to blood lineage. But if he was not born with a silver spoon between his lips, he was certainly familiar with the corridors of power. His passage through Oxford and the RAF to parliament, where he arrived as a Labour MP in 1950, had been smoothed in advance by the benefits of connection, education and freedom from want.

In the Commons he took his distance from the left, although he thought of himself as left of centre. He was never part of the Bevanite group or its revolts. True, he was heavily involved in the anti-colonial movement, and with Brockway and others founded the Movement for Colonial Freedom in 1954. In the same year he also helped to found the H-Bomb National Committee to campaign against the development of nuclear weapons by Britain, and to call for a summit conference on disarmament. But, arguing for the traditional moderate Labour position of disarmament through negotiation, he opposed unilateralism, and stayed on the fringes of the struggle that erupted in the Labour Party in the early sixties on the twin themes of nuclear weapons and public ownership.

In 1960 when Bevan died there was little to indicate that in 1980 he would tell the party:

> '. . . the election of May 1979 marked a real watershed for the labour movement as well as for the nation.
>
> To put it in plain language, forty years of experience of trying to pretend that welfare capitalism was possible, successful and permanent, and could melt away the conflict of interest between Labour and Capital have proved it cannot be done . . . what we are witnessing is the re-opening of the class struggle.'[1]

Yet by the time he made this speech he had evolved from one of the key figures in Wilson's 1964 government to the most detested enemy of the British establishment. As Industry Minister in 1974 he had found himself the object of a single-minded and vitriolic attack which led to his being driven from the Department and his policies anathematised by Wilson. He was branded as the inspirer of a new, dangerous and extremist movement in the Labour Party – a rank and file movement of such passion and power that, against all odds and opposition, it carried him to the brink of the deputy leadership, throwing the Labour Party into its deepest crisis since the war.

This reflects profound changes in British society, comparable perhaps with the turmoil that destroyed the Liberal Party and launched the Labour Party. Two facts point to this conclusion.

Firstly, the Benn movement, though a minority current, is nonetheless deeply *popular*. It has swept the constituency Labour Parties. It won over two million votes in the unions. In December 1981 a poll indicated that forty per cent of Labour voters in the unions wanted Benn to continue his campaign in the Labour Party. Wherever he speaks, Benn attracts record audiences. This is a new, mass, popular social movement.

Secondly, establishment reaction has been quite out of the ordinary. Benn is not just disapproved of. He is anathematised. His views are not just wrong; they are evil. Not one national newspaper supports them. Even Labour's old left wing has risked steps against them that could destroy the party.

When Labour swept to power in 1945 the *Evening Standard* called it a 'perhaps natural desire on the part of the people, not so much for a change of government, as for one of party and personalities' and said it should be 'accepted loyally by one and all'. Bennism is seen differently. It has become a *heresy*. It is seen as so dangerous that it is not to be debated but rooted out and destroyed. Such intolerance towards the passionate views of millions of people can only mean that their beliefs are deeply subversive of the existing social order.

How has this happened? A great error is made by those – whether of the left or the right – who explain Benn's role in terms of his personality, fire, eloquence, lust for power or thirst for acclaim. He gives expression to immensely powerful social forces, and we can understand him only by understanding them. This book aims to study them through the prism of their impact on his thoughts and actions.

Benn deserves personal credit for having raised questions which have been out of the mainstream of British politics for more than a century. These questions also deserve answers.

This book does not accept Benn's answers. Revolutionary socialism and revolutionary democracy – which, it will be argued, as one and the same – have long been asking the same questions, and, we think, coming up with better answers. But Benn's achievement is to have re-introduced these questions to a mass British public. In order to reach its own answers, the socialist movement should return the service in its best possible democratic tradition, by *understanding* his questions, his answers, and how he reached them.

1. The Enemy Without

Ah, Love! Could thou and I with Fate conspire
    To grasp this sorry scheme of things entire,
Would we not shatter it to bits and then
    Remould it closer to the heart's desire!

Edward FitzGerald *Rubaiyyat of Omar Khayyam*

On 16 October 1964 Harold Wilson formed the first Labour Government in thirteen years. In a second election in March 1966 he was to turn Labour's narrow four-seat margin into a thumping overall majority of 97. Labour was pledged to sweep away the dead wood from the boardrooms and the cobwebs from the corridors of power. It was going to bulldoze away the relics of thirteen years of Tory misrule and pull Britain into the twentieth century.

The 1964 manifesto caught this mood, which infected the Benns along with much of the rest of Britain. Caroline, Tony's wife, had suggested the title 'The New Britain', which was expanded to the more long-winded but successful 'Let's go with Labour for the New Britain'.

Both Wilson and Benn sought to unite the party around a vision of dynamic, high-technology modernisation. 'We are redefining and restating our socialism in terms of the scientific revolution', Wilson told the 1963 conference, 'The Britain that is going to be forged in the white heat of this revolution will be no place for restrictive practices or outdated methods'.[1]

Benn was heavily committed to the new government and its vision of the future. Kept from the Commons until October 1963 by a three-year fight to renounce his hereditary peerage, he was anxious to re-enter parliamentary politics. A rising star in the Labour Party, he had come third in the last elections to the constituency section of the National Executive Committee with 725,000 votes, and narrowly missed election to the Shadow Cabinet. In December 1963 he became Wilson's unofficial speech-writer, and after the general election received his first government appointment as Postmaster-General.

It was not a Cabinet post, but his disappointment was short lived. In 1966 left-wing union leader Frank Cousins resigned from the Ministry of Technology – the furnace room of Wilson's revolution – in protest against incomes legislation. At Wilson's invitation, it was Benn who took his place.

It wasn't just Benn and Wilson who were committed to this new vision. The *Economist* came out for Labour, expressing business exasperation with the Tory Party. Its leader Alec Douglas-Home, dragged from the Lords to salvage it from a succession of unsavoury scandals, seemed to symbolise everything out-of-date and class-ridden in the country. More importantly, business circles saw the need to orient trade and investment away from the old empire and towards Europe. Macmillan had failed to get Britain into the EEC precisely because of the empire and the 'special relationship' with the USA. Labour was better placed to make the shift. Years of social spending financed by overseas income had allowed a powerful and well-organised labour movement to flourish almost unchallenged. A Labour government, governing on the twin, apparently classless, themes of technology and modernisation and with trade union support, seemed an ideal instrument for bringing about change.

These themes appealed also to Benn. In 1967 he explained to the American Chamber of Commerce that:

> 'Technology challenges governments, whether capitalist, communist, or socialist, and industry whether publicly or privately owned in such a direct fashion that the common interest uniting them is stronger and more important than the disagreements which divide them.
>
> Every society will seek to express this common interest in its own way and in the light of its own history. Here in Britain we start with a mixed economy, and we shall have one as far ahead as I can see.
>
> We must therefore make a mixed economy work. Make it successful; make it competitive; look to it to create the wealth we need to do the things we want to do.'[2]

But hopes in the new government were soon dashed. Instead of opening a new era, it began the slow trek back to the thirties.

Underlying trends of declining competitiveness and economic stagnation continued unchecked. Between 1965 and 1970 company profitability, after tax, fell from 6.4 per cent to only 4.9 per cent. From 1964 until 1969 the rate of growth of productivity was only 3.4 per cent, whilst in the EEC 'big five' it rose from 4.8 per cent to 5.9 per cent. Britain's share of world exports fell in the same period from 14.4 per cent to 10.8 per cent, and import penetration of British markets rose from 11.9 per cent to 14.8 per cent.[3]

Labour faced recurring balance of payments problems, but accepted City wisdom on the need for a strong pound – to the benefit of the old imperial clique of importers and overseas investors, and to the detriment of exporters and domestic investors. When, during the 1967 sterling crisis, it bowed to the inevitable and devalued, it was forced to deflate to ensure that profits did not suffer.

In the wake of devaluation, social spending was cut by £1 billion, and unemployment doubled to 600,000. Benn commented to the 1968 conference:

> 'We underestimated the time it would take to create the economic resources to back up our social commitments . . . I assure you that anyone observing . . . what is happening in British industry today would, if he were open-minded at all, be converted to the need for public enterprise and public accountability.'[4]

On foreign policy the government was a great disappointment. It dashed the hopes of a generation of CND campaigners by strengthening Britain's nuclear arsenal. It backed every turn and twist of American foreign policy in Vietnam and, as Benn later commented, failed to end Britain's presence east of Suez in spite of its manifesto commitment. Labour's foreign secretary, Michael Stewart, became a particular target for the growing anti-Vietnam war movement, which by 1968 was organising 100,000 strong demonstrations in London.

The party, which had opposed immigration controls as a matter of deepest principle under Gaitskell, bowed to ugly new racialist moods in the electorate, and strengthened Tory restrictions on immigration. It responded to the civil rights struggle in Ireland as every British administration has always done – by sending in the troops.

These moves alienated it from a new generation, whose political ideas were given shape and hope by wars of liberation, by the 'Prague Spring' in Czechoslovakia, and by the French 'May events' of 1968. A dramatic decline in individual membership of the Labour Party was accompanied by a rapid growth of far left organisations. New autonomous movements of youth, black people, women and students were bypassing it.

Most destructive of all was a rift with the unions which opened scarcely eighteen months after Wilson took office, and finally broke the administration.

In 1966 Wilson launched a vicious witch-hunting attack on the seamen's strike, which he claimed was politically inspired by Communists. This antagonised rank and file militants who had ended right-wing domination of the huge engineering and transport unions, and whose leaders refused to go along with the increasingly anti-working class direction of government policy. Wage restraint was the issue behind Frank Cousins' resignation from MinTech in 1966, setting the stage for a damaging split between party and unions, and eventually in the party's own ranks.

Barbara Castle's White Paper *In Place of Strife* proposed statutory government powers to curb unofficial strikes. It advocated compulsory strike ballots, 'cooling off' periods, and financial penalties for disobedience. It was defeated and withdrawn after a year of campaigning by the rank-and-file based Liaison Committee for the Defence of Trade Unions. This united behind it most of the left-wing, trade union leaders, 53 MPs, and enough grass-roots support to organise Britain's first political general strike since the war. The government which had set out to re-unite the nation had proved unable to hold its own ranks together. Its political will was broken and its election defeat in June 1970 almost inevitable.

Democracy: first encounters

Benn's first term in office affected him profoundly. As the Bevanites marched rightward, he marched leftward. This was to become typical. 'It may seem strange', he says,

> 'that a cabinet minister should be radicalised while in office. It would be more usual for a radical MP to be converted to respectability the moment he receives his seals of office. For me it was different.'

Why and how did his conversion begin to take place? A constant theme in his own accounts is a preoccupation, not with the Bevanite themes of prosperity and material wellbeing, but with political democracy.

The 1964-70 government caught him in the same crisis as all Labour's parliamentarians. The economic prosperity on which traditional welfare state policies were founded had collapsed. Wilson – who had been one of the three original Bevanite Ministers – concluded that Labour's sails should be trimmed to cope with the economic winds. But Benn saw a democratically elected government being denied the right to carry out the policies on which it was elected. If economic circumstance stood in the way of these policies then the answer was to change not the policies but the economic circumstances.

He was prepared for this by an experience which he considers critical to his personal evolution: his struggle to renounce the peerage.

Churchill had sought to seal his wartime coalition by boosting Labour's very low representation in the House of Lords. One of his four choices was his former colleague on the Liberal benches of the 1906 Parliament, William Wedgwood Benn. William had joined the Labour Party in 1926 and served as Secretary of State for India in the ill-fated MacDonald administration of 1929–31. Churchill had him created Viscount Stansgate. The title was hereditary.

Benn succeeded automatically to the title and its attendant place in the House of Lords on his father's death in 1960. By law he could not serve in both Houses. Unlike many Labour leaders for whom a peerage has served as a reward for a life of compromise, Benn neither sought this honour nor took it. Now that it barred him from the Commons, the battle began in earnest.

The fight had many strange side-effects – not the least of which was to bring Lords Home and Hailsham into the Commons. But for Benn the most important consequence was the doubt it raised about the true nature of British parliamentary democracy.

'Like a test card going through a computer system,' he said,

> 'it tested the House of Commons and its Committees, the House of Lords and its Committees, the Crown insofar as it was involved, the press, local government, the Labour Party, the Conference, the Constituency . . . it was a most extraordinary way of learning how the British Constitution worked and where power resided, and I learned a lot of things that shocked me very much, particularly the ideas of those who ran parliamentary government – I learned that they were not particularly democratic at all.'[5]

In asking for the right *not* to be a peer, Benn was asking *for* the right to be an MP. He was thus asking for the right of the people of Bristol South East to send to the House of Commons the person they chose to be their representative. He described himself as 'not a reluctant peer but a persistent commoner.'

On 29 November 1960 his constituency party backed his stand overwhelmingly, and 10,537 of his constituents signed a petition protesting that 'they may be unjustly denied their right of free choice in the member they have elected to represent them in the present Parliament'.[6]

After a stormy Commons debate, Benn was barred from the House and denied a hearing before it. Fifteen Tory MPs voted against their government, and MP Charles Pannell declared that he could 'almost sniff and smell fire and think we are in the Reichstag'[7] – a somewhat misplaced historical analogy which nevertheless expressed the passions roused by the issue.

A fresh election was held. Benn was unanimously reselected by his constituency party. The election result, announced on 5 May 1961, gave him 23,275 votes against the 10,231 of his Tory opponent Malcolm St Clair – more than doubling his 1959 majority.

On 8 May he tried to enter the House again. He was barred again. 'Are you instructed to prevent me from entering by physical force if necessary?', he asked the doorkeeper. 'I am, sir', came the reply.[8] Rejecting Benn's lengthy and detailed case, the election court set up to determine Malcolm St Clair's claim to take his seat in the Commons found that 'The hereditary principle is still firmly embodied in the constitution'.

In a conflict between the elective principle of the Commons, and the hereditary principle of the Lords, the former gave way.

For Benn this called into question the representative nature of the Commons. Was this just the tip of the iceberg, and were there other, more sinister unaccountable centres of power lurking in the background of political life? These were the questions he asked himself during the two further years it took to complete his battle and resume his seat in the Commons.

Democracy and economy

They remained at the back of his mind as he began his first term of office in Her Majesty's government. As conflict grew between this government and those to whom it was in theory accountable, he became more and more worried that the obstacles to democracy might lie, not just with a few quaint anachronisms of the British Constitution, but at the heart of the system as it now stood. He gave public voice to these fears at the Welsh Council of Labour in Llandudno in 1968, just after the May events in France. 'What about parliamentary democracy?' he asked,

> 'can we assume that it will go on, in exactly the same form as we now have it, for ever and ever? I very much doubt it.
>
> It would be foolish to assume that people will be satisfied for much longer with a system that confines their national political role to the marking of a ballot paper with a single cross once every five years.
>
> People want a much greater say. That certainly explains some of the student protests against the authoritarian hierarchies in some of our universities and their sense of isolation from the problems of real life.
>
> Much of the industrial unrest – especially in unofficial strikes – stems from workers' resentment and their sense of exclusion from the decision making process, whether by their employers or, sometimes, by their union leaders.
>
> Frustration, too, provides much of the driving force for nationalism in Wales and Scotland among those who want to participate more fully in policy-making.
>
> Even the black power movement is an indication that coloured immigrants are not prepared to rely entirely on white liberals to champion their cause and are determined to assume a more direct responsibility for securing their rights.'[9]

Benn was evolving a critique of the whole of parliamentary

democracy as practised today in Britain. He put forward the idea of a new kind of democracy – a popular, participating democracy – in which parliament would remain at the centre, but people at all levels would be directly involved in decision-making and in running their lives. Popular government, shared government, open government: these were his new slogans.

> 'The danger of parliamentary democracy – if it is presented as if it were nothing more than the achievement of an elected monarchy – is that it retains the arrogance of the benevolent despot and seeks to cloak the elected MP with something of the Divine Right once reserved for royal personages. At its worst, it still keeps the citizen at arm's length from the business of decision-making and bullies him into believing that the ballot box is the last word in participation.
>
> However attractive this idea may be, it won't do because it won't work any more. The game is up and we have to think the whole thing out again.'[10]

This emerging democratic vision had no immediate or early impact on his economic policy, which if anything moved to the right during his first years in office. Indeed he supported the first draft of *In Place of Strife*. It was only when Wilson's remedies called into being a movement of energetic and popular resistance that he was forced to re-examine the assumptions behind these remedies, and seek the underlying reasons for the failure of government policy. This process of reflection only bore fruit after the fall of the Wilson government.

The core of his policy at MinTech was therefore the belief that government should create the best conditions for industrial profitability. It should do this by stimulating research and development, and then by persuading, or cajoling industry into applying the results.

To the first end the Ministry of Technology greatly expanded the National Research and Development Corporation together with government-controlled research establishments. It presided over a spirit of scientific renaissance which fired the enthusiasm of a generation of researchers.

The media made Benn a symbol of naive faith in technology. After he championed the Hovercraft they labelled him 'Hover Benn' and tried to saddle him with the image of boyscout enthusiasm combined with total lack of practical business understanding.

In spite of this the Ministry chalked up some impressive achievements. Its problems lay not in the development of new technology but in persuading industry to apply it. Although Benn held that government should enter a close relationship with industry, he expected the mechanisms of the market and private incentive to play the central role. This was probably the high point of his commitment to the ideal of the mixed economy. In a speech at Imperial College he argued that:

> 'there will always be arguments about how profit should be distributed as between customer, employer, workers and the community [but] the profitability of a mixed economy is an essential prerequisite of economic growth and commercial success.'

The Ministry grew a gigantic apparatus. At its height it commanded a staff of 39,600 with a budget of £2.5 billion. Yet it became increasingly obvious that this wasn't enough. Despite all the opportunities offered it, British industry was not investing in new technology. Indeed it was not investing in Britain. For every £100 which British employers put into industry under the Wilson government, their French counterparts put in £238, the Japanese £218, and the Americans £395. 'Industrial investment in the private sector', Benn commented later, 'has been consistently lower than everyone in management and labour has known to be necessary if Britain was to remain a major industrial power'.[11]

The first signs of what was later to be known as de-industrialisation began to show: the decline of manufacturing industry at the expense of finance and other services. Ironically, in spite of the outcry against excessive state spending, employment by national and local government had remained fixed at little over 1.4 million between 1951 and 1971. But employment in the finance and banking sector rose from around 450 thousand in 1951, to 550 thousand in 1961 and over 950 thousand in 1971. Nor was banking particularly involved, as were its Japanese and German counterparts, with developing domestic industry. Japanese studies indicated that the crucial difference was the willingness of their own banks to issue long-term finance to domestic industry. Indeed the City provoked even Wilson by its refusal to advance long-term loans to

British industry. Manufacturing employment proved to have reached a postwar peak at 9.2m in 1966, and began now to plummet. It fell to 8.8m in 1969. A scant ten years later it was to plunge to 7.2m.[12]

Benn's first reaction to this problem would hardly be recognised as his today. Along with Wilson he was convinced that *size* was the great obstacle to progress. 1965-70 was the age of the government-inspired merger. Paradoxically the man who has in recent years been identified with resisting the big and impersonal probably did most to promote it. 'One of the principal objects of MinTech is to try and bring about larger units in British engineering industry', he explained in 1968,

> 'Technology imposes an inexorable scale in our economic life . . . we want a climate favourable to large companies if we are to stand up to the competition from across the Atlantic.'

This view swung him for a period in favour of admission to the European Economic Community. When Macmillan first applied for entry Benn had argued against it on a cogent and comprehensive basis as laissez-faire, cold war, protectionist and undemocratic. But now he felt that the need to develop large-scale technology outweighed these arguments. Speaking in Bonn in February 1968, after the Labour government's application, he argued that:

> 'it was partly through our analysis of the impact of technology upon industry that we came to the historic decision to apply for full membership of the European Economic Community.
>
> Britain may have been slow to see the importance of the European Community. But I believe she was the first to see that technology imposes upon all of us its inexorable logic of scale . . . The political opposition to our membership will be ineffective because the nationalistic arguments upon which it is based are becoming increasingly irrelevant.'[13]

Yet the very effects of the policy showed its weakness. His biographer remarks:

> 'Between 1965-70 the leading 100 manufacturing companies' share of output rose from 37 per cent to 45 per cent but the merger movement of the late sixties had little to do with industrial efficiency. None of the mergers led to either increased investment or expansion. The majority were caused by an unfavourable economic

> climate which inflated asset values and depressed trading profits and share prices.'[14]

Far from stimulating new investment in expanding areas, government intervention was merely propping up declining industries whose failure was the result of decades of neglect. More ominous still was the growing difference in class reaction to the worsening economic climate.

This was brought to a head by the sterling crisis of 1967 and the devaluation it provoked. Industry and banking both insisted on cuts in public spending – above all on the social services – and on wage restraint. They resisted government intervention in industry, and bitterly fought Benn's proposed Industrial Expansion Bill of 1968, which aimed to rationalise government powers of intervention.

This Bill was a mild proposal. Benn doggedly insisted that:

> 'There is little disagreement between the two sides of the House on the need for government financial support for industry . . . a doctrinal objection to all intervention is wholly unpracticable . . . Those who criticise the idea of government interference have a responsibility to provide an alternative answer to this question.'[15]

Yet, significantly, it was attacked not only by the CBI and the Tories but by Callaghan himself. The terms of the debate were soon to become much more familiar. Sir Keith Joseph led off the attack, arguing that:

> 'We wish to repeat and repeat again that the public sector is inherently likely to be more inefficient than the private sector because it is not subject to the discipline of the market and because in many cases it is subsidised.'[16]

Benn had met his first hardline challenge from what was later to become the new Tory right.

Investment and control

This highlighted the difficulty of using orthodox methods. Keynesian ideals, to which Labour subscribed, dictated that while the government could interfere with the market within a 'mixed economy' to affect *demand*, it could not regulate *supply* too closely. This was a euphemism for asserting that the government should not deprive the owners of capital of the right to make their own investment decisions.

This was not just an ideological point; it went to the heart of the way in which owners of capital were affected by competition. They had to be able to move capital from one place to another in order to seek the highest rate of profit. If they could not do so, not merely would their returns be lower, but they risked being dwarfed and swallowed by other capitals. From their point of view it was essential to their self-interest that the freedom of capital movement be maintained. They justified this to society by claiming that free competition produced efficiency – somewhat hypocritically, Benn felt, since capital was now highly monopolised.

Rather than confront capital's violent opposition to any restrictions on its movement, Labour's Keynesian tradition was that of the 'carrot and stick' – using selective state incentives to encourage investment decisions in society's interests. But it studiously avoided any *compulsory* allocation of investment resources in case it lowered business confidence.

This now became a double millstone around its neck. It was very reluctant to attack the finance sector, which commanded the most liquid resources and hence the most ready power. Labour needed these for social spending, and could be easily blackmailed by the threat of their withdrawal. But, because the finance sector was geared to overseas activity, Labour could not weaken the old imperial habits, based on the strong pound. It left devaluation until the last minute and took no steps to nationalise the banks.

When Labour did devalue, it was forced to attack working people. The aim of the 1967 devaluation was to lower export prices and raise import prices, in the hope that less would be bought abroad and more sold abroad, bringing the balance of payments into line. But this could only happen if working people were made to shoulder the costs.

The immediate effect of a fall in the pound was, of course, to raise the import bill by raising prices. If workers had responded by forcing up wages, domestic producers would have lost all the advantage of increased demand for their goods, there would have been no incentive for increased domestic investment and the result could have been an inflationary spiral followed by a collapse of the currency.

Indeed, so strong were the pressures on the government to deal with the balance of payments by means other than attacking the rich, that a Cabinet crisis erupted around the demand, fiercely fought by Benn and promoted by Brown, Callaghan, Healey, Walker, Thomson, Gunter and Crosland, for the resumption of arms sales to South Africa.

Matters were not improved by the fact that the government had to resort to international borrowing, prompting Wilson to his furious outbursts against the demands of the 'Gnomes of Zurich'. But the 'gnomes' were only stating the conditions which Britain's own domestic investors needed to reap the benefits of devaluation.

There was, of course, an alternative, to which Benn now began to be drawn. This was to seek some *other means* of directing and controlling investment – either by the state, or indeed by workers themselves. And in fact the notion that workers should have a say in the effects of investment decisions now surfaced – as the post-devaluation package began to push the unemployment figures up.

Benn began to confront the angry reactions of the trade union movement. The rationalisation and merger of GEC was one of the achievements of government policy. Yet in 1969 stewards at GEC's Napier factory in Liverpool, angrily reacting to its proposed closure, made the first occupation attempt of postwar times.

At the same time resistance to wage restraint and restrictions on the unions was growing, expressed in the campaign against *In Place of Strife* and the Liaison Committee for the Defence of the Trade Unions.

Benn's idea that technology could forge a common bond between workers, government and industry did not stand up in practice. Conflict between workers and employers was growing. Economic necessity seemed to give the government no option but to side with the employers. Yet at the same time the employers were sharpening their attacks on the government. The spirit of tripartite endeavour – if such a spirit had ever existed – was giving way to a three-way split.

The implications for democracy were very uncomfortable. In the name of profitability, industry was forcing the government to take on, oppose, defeat and impoverish the very people that had elected it – people who in fact made up a majority of the population. At the same time, industry itself refused to recognise public interest, denied the economy the investment needed to revitalise it, and flouted the government's plans.

Rich, privileged and powerful minority interests stood in the way of the needs and democratically expressed desires of the majority.

Benn concluded that these minority interests had begun to constitute an unaccountable power of such magnitude and strength as to be a major threat to democracy. In 1973 he outlined this conclusion to an audience of businessmen at a conference organised by the *Financial Times*.

> 'I have been looking through those institutions represented here today at this lunch, in order to get some idea of the power of this very audience . . .
>
> The banks represented here alone have total assets worth at least £65 billion. Add the other financial institutions and the figures rise to about £95 billion. This is about twice the Gross National Product of the United Kingdom and four or five times the total sum raised in taxation and spent by the British government each year. The Labour Party must ask what effect all this power will have on the nature of our democracy . . .
>
> We tried to work by the indirect method using a system of negative controls, and huge public subsidies to try and inject the national interest into boardroom thinking . . . But our experience, and their experience, has convinced us that policies based on the carrot and the stick are not adequate . . . Such policies cannot catch up with the chronic problem created by years of under-investment in Britain . . . Economic power is getting too concentrated; is being abused; is threatening democracy, is preserving a pattern of power and privilege which is grand for the minority who enjoy it but not good for the rest.
>
> All this is bound to lead to a public demand for fundamental reform.'[17]

The enemies of democracy were no longer concentrated in the fusty corridors of aristocratic privilege. They were assembled in front of him as he spoke: the directors, shareholders, and bankers of British industry.

2. The New Politics

> O thou powers of England, though thou hast promised to make this people a free people, yet hast thou so handled the matter through thy self-seeking humour that thou hast wrapped us up in more bondage, and oppression lies heavier upon us; not only bringing thy fellow creatures, the commoners, to a morsel of bread, but by confounding all sorts of people by thy government of doing and undoing.
>
> First, thou hast made the people to take a covenant and oaths to endeavour a reformation and to bring in liberty every man in his place; and yet while a man is in pursuing of that covenant, he is imprisoned and oppressed by thy officers, courts, and justices, so called.
>
> Thou hast made ordinances to cast down oppressing, popish, episcopal, self-willed and prerogative laws; yet we see that self-will and prerogative power is the great standing law that rules all in action, and others in words . . .
>
> And all this because the people stand to maintain an universal liberty and freedom, which is not only our birthright which our maker gave us, but which thou hast promised to restore unto us, from under the former oppressing powers that are gone before, and which likewise we have bought with our money, in taxes, free-quarter and bloodshed; all of which sums thou hast received at our hands, and yet thou hast not given us our bargain.
>
> Gerrard Winstanley, *The True Levellers' Standard Advanced*

On 19 June 1970 Edward Heath became Prime Minister in a Tory government with a 30-seat majority. The foundations of Benn's socialism were laid in the four years that followed.

His ideas on the need for a popular, participatory democracy had been evolving since 1968. Relieved of the responsibilities of office, he could concentrate his energies on a public study of the causes of Labour's failure, and on the painstaking work of charting a new socialist course.

This was no academic exercise. The years 1970-74 were the stormiest since 1926, ending with an event unprecedented in British history: the fall of an elected government in the face of mass industrial opposition. Benn began to feel that an alternative to the strategy of the 1964-70 government was being offered by the very movements and struggles on which Wilson had turned his back. The people themselves had to be the source of change. The industrial struggles, autonomous movements, and campaigns which had mushroomed under the 1964-69 government showed how this could be achieved.

'How can we give responsibility', he asked a Fabian audience in November 1971, 'except to people who are already demanding it?'

> 'This brings me straight to the major theme I want to develop in this lecture. It is very simple, very old, but for all that, very radical. It is this: we shall never change society unless we start to do it ourselves by directly challenging the unaccountable power now exercised over us, and prepare to exercise it responsibly ourselves, exactly as our forefathers did by demanding the vote in the nineteenth century.'[1]

He sought a role for direct action in a parliamentary democracy. 'The credibility gap in British politics', he went on, '. . . does not arise from excessive promises made in policy fields'.

> 'It arises from a wholly incredible claim made for the whole system, which cannot achieve what it claims to achieve, just because it focuses too exclusively on parliament and virtually ignores the people's role in social change.
>
> This is not an appeal for violent revolution or even systematic and sustained civil disobedience. In Britain we don't need them. It is an appeal for a strategy of change from below to make the parliamentary system serve the people instead of serving the vanity of parliamentarians: an appeal for popular democracy. Indeed the greatest achievements of the left came about in this way.
>
> Historically, when democratic pressures from below were strong enough, the system worked just because the people on top accepted them. This is how the British people won free trade unionism, got the vote, the welfare state and the health service, and why we are tackling the environment and thinking afresh about women's rights.
>
> This being so, why should it be regarded as so unacceptable

> that parliamentarians interpret their representative function as meaning that they should accept those pressures and respond to them? . . . Democratic change starts with a struggle at the bottom and ends with a peaceful parliamentary victory at the top. This is what I want to call Popular Democracy.'[2]

But how was the idea of popular democracy to be transformed into a living reality? Benn grappled with three problems: how to resolve the constitutional relation between direct and parliamentary action; how the party and unions could work together under a future Labour government; and how the policy objectives of such a government could be defined.

The end of a consensus

He was by now convinced that a struggle for popular democracy implied a struggle for socialism. 'The Ministry of Technology made me a socialist', he later said. It had taught him that democracy was under attack because the owners of wealth and privilege, in the face of an economic crisis of their own making, defended themselves at the expense of working people and their families – the great majority of the population. Democracy therefore called for a siege of the multinational barons and their Whitehall courtiers. They had to be made to relinquish control of the great resources of power at their command. This power had to be shared with the ordinary people and their elected government. Benn wanted to revitalise one of the oldest, yet most revolutionary ideas in the labour movement: that democracy demands socialism, and socialism demands democracy.

He explored these ideas in a Fabian pamphlet, written directly after Labour's election defeat and published in September 1970. Entitled *The New Politics* and subtitled 'A Socialist Reconnaissance', it argued that traditional Labour policies had been brought to grief by a deeper social crisis than a mere temporary economic hiccough. Something in the fabric of society was changing which would force Labour to question all its traditions, methods and tactics. His analysis was confirmed when the new administration hit the labour movement like an icy shower.

The real Edward Heath of 1970 bore little resemblance to the genial Heath image of the eighties. His government made a radical break with the policies of both the Wilson government and the preceding Macmillan/Home government. State money was to be withdrawn from industry's 'lame ducks'; draconian new anti-union legislation was to be introduced and public services were to be slashed. 'Selsdon Man' was going to drag meandering, featherbedded Britain into the Common Market, let the cold winds of competition blow round its feeble legs, and bring down the full wrath of the law on the heads of industry's union wreckers.

The unions reacted first with shock; then with outrage; and finally with mayhem. Their left wing had been greatly strengthened by the arrival of Hugh Scanlon and Jack Jones at the head of the two biggest unions, the AUEW and the TGWU. The stewards' movement had built up confidence and militancy through the 'wage drift' struggles of the fifties and sixties – factory by factory negotiations in which shopfloor organisation had developed into a finely-honed weapon. Trade union membership, now topping ten million, was higher than ever before and there had been a remarkable surge of unionisation amongst white collar administrative, technical and clerical workers.

Within a year workers at Upper Clyde Shipbuilders (UCS) organised the first postwar factory occupation. Occupations averaged one every fortnight from then on. The miners invented the flying picket, rediscovered the mass picket, and showed that they could take on and defeat thousands of police when they closed down Saltley Gate coking depot in the course of the 1972 dispute. Mass industrial action reduced Heath's anti-union legislation to tatters in mid-1972. Finally, in an all-out attempt to break the miners' strike of 1974 – an open challenge to the government's income policy and implicitly to the government itself – Heath imposed a three-day working week on the whole of industry but failed to stop the strike. He called an election on the issue of 'who rules?' – and lost.

Both the Tories and the unions had rediscovered class struggle on the grand scale.

Benn was convinced that these developments signalled irreversible changes in British politics. It forced everyone into a major exercise in rethinking. 'The Tories went back to Adam Smith, the Labour Party to Clause IV, and the Archbishop of

Canterbury to the ten commandments,'[3] he said later.

As he saw it, the Wilson and Heath governments had exploded the myth, carefully fostered by Macmillan, that a free enterprise British economy possessed the necessary resources and status for an endless expansion of wealth in which all could share. 'You've never had it so good', was Macmillan's rallying cry. It was intended to frighten voters with an image of Labour as the party of austerity and regimentation, playing on postwar memories of rationing and state bureaucracy. Vote Labour, said Macmillan, and the horn of plenty will run dry. In reality that was already happening. Wilson had inherited a bankrupt economy. Heath was obliged to launch a programme of shock anti-working class treatment because his backers no longer commanded the resources to dispense reforms or concessions without serious damage to their own interests.

Benn argued that this signalled the end of the 'postwar consensus' within which both Tory and Labour governments had worked. He credited Heath with realism:

> 'In a way I admire Heath for confronting at Selsdon and afterwards the reality of the situation which was that you couldn't patch it [the postwar consensus] any more. You had in his view to deal with the root cause of British weakness or decline and you had to do it by rolling back the power of the trade unions and by introducing more competition.'[4]

However, although Benn could endorse Heath's realism, in no way did he endorse his actions, which he saw as the naked imposition of narrow ruling class interests on the nation as a whole. On the contrary, Heath's policy constituted a fundamental challenge to democracy. This was epitomised for Benn in the process of entry into the Common Market, which Heath pushed through with immoderate haste inside eighteen months.

Benn swung into wholehearted opposition to EEC entry. He fought it to some extent on foreign policy grounds: it was part and parcel of a cold war, militaristic structure of alliances. But his most sustained attack centred on the constitutional implications of Heath's actions.

Heath was carrying out a basic constitutional change *without consulting the people*. Parliament, which ought to take its mandate from the people, had surrendered rights which were not in its gift.

The sovereignty of the people over parliament meant that they should be given the ultimate decision. Benn developed a campaign for a referendum on EEC entry which was eventually written into the Labour Party's manifesto, and in 1975 constitutional history was made when this referendum was actually carried out – ironically playing a decisive role in Benn's defeat in the Labour Cabinet of the day.

Just as important as the manner in which Heath had sought entry into the EEC, however, was the nature of the EEC itself. Benn argued that the Treaty of Rome meant that parliament was ceding the right to make and execute laws to an unaccountable Brussels bureaucracy, which the people of Britain could not discipline or sack. This threatened the basic fabric of democracy. 'If the British people are herded into a federation against their will', he said to the Commons, 'the whole fabric of our society will be threatened:'

> '*First*, we shall find ourselves governed by laws we did not make and cannot change;
> *Second*, we shall find ourselves taxed by people we did not elect and cannot remove;
> *Third*, we shall find ourselves locked into economic policies that may harm us and cannot be altered because they were devised to meet the needs of others;
> *Fourth*, we shall be governed by European bureaucrats, elected by no-one, for whom Ministers are only needed as a rubber stamp;
> *Fifth*, we may find ourselves sucked into a European military machine with its own nuclear weapons shared by France, Britain and possibly Germany, over whose use the British people will have no control at all.
>
> When the British people wake up to realise what is happening, there will be a veritable explosion of rage directed not just against Mr Heath, but against any MP in any party who joins a conspiracy to destroy 700 years of parliamentary democratic self-government by stealth.
>
> The strength of parliament has always rested on the foundations of public faith in it.
>
> Take that faith away and you destroy institutions of self-government that generations of British people have laboured to create.
>
> Once the people discover that parliament has given away the people's rights, then there will be no logical argument for retaining the system.'[5]

Heath's offensive was a class offensive. 'When historians come to write about this period of British history', he said on the eve of Heath's downfall,

> 'Mr Heath will certainly be credited with having awakened people, who had never thought about class before, to what class means, and how it related to their own experience. This will greatly increase support for the unions and the Labour Party.'[6]

Heath served, not the electorate, but the small minority of bankers and shareholders who demanded the trade union movement's destruction. Benn considered this was leading to an attempt to take from the unions rights so basic that they stood above law itself.

In July 1972 five dockers were sent to jail by Sir John Donaldson for breaches of the new Industrial Relations Act. The imprisonment provoked a storm of industrial action and protest, leading to a general strike call by the TUC, endorsed by Labour's National Executive Committee. The freeing of the 'Pentonville Five', as they became known, was a turning point in the life of the government. Again, Benn saw the issues involved as of basic constitutional significance. What attitude should be taken towards a law which, although passed by a democratically elected government, breached democratic principles which no government ought to challenge?

Speaking on the eve of the Annual Tolpuddle Martyrs' Demonstration and Rally in August 1972, he compared the imprisoned dockers to the six Dorset men who had been transported in 1834 for trying to form a union. 'For centuries', he said, 'Britain's democratic liberties have been won and upheld with the help of men and women who stood up for their beliefs and took the consequences.'

> 'The right to worship freely, to organise trade unions, to vote – for men and women – in Britain were all won against powerful people who sought to maintain their privileges by stirring public fears about anarchy whenever anyone challenged these privileges. That is what the government are now trying to do.
>
> The British people are the most law-abiding people in the world. It would be quite wrong for anyone to tell others to break the law. But we cannot forget that, in the end, each man is answerable to his own conviction as to what is right and wrong. If a man's

conscience lands him in jail the bars that keep him there also imprison part of all our freedoms.
The law which has put these men in prison is an evil law, drawn up by a government which hates the trade unions, and is being enforced by lawyers who have no experience of the problems of working people and their families.'[7]

These actions called into account the constitutional authority of the government. Benn believed Heath aimed to create an atmosphere in which strong, near dictatorial measures against the unions would be imposed without resistance. With considerable foresight, he argued in a draft Shadow Cabinet paper written during these events:

> 'It is widely believed that if a voluntary policy for controlling wages is not acceptable the government will quickly move to a statutory policy. Then if industrial disputes take place, they will switch at once to a 'Who Governs Britain' campaign directed against the trade union movement, holding them responsible for unemployment, inflation and for undermining law and order . . . they are building for the moment when picketing, or even an angry strike meeting could be shown as part of a pattern of anarchy. From then it is easy to demand strong counter-measures of a kind that 'only Mr Heath can provide'.
>
> It is easy to see why the government are adopting this policy . . . almost every policy on which they were elected has had to be abandoned, with the exception of their policy on the Common Market which has not won majority support . . . The theme of anarchy, deliberately raising public anxiety and putting the blame on the trade unions is undoubtedly their best bet as they see it.
>
> It is, therefore, a political campaign directed against them that the trade union movement now has to face, and we are deeply involved. If we are to respond effectively we shall have to re-examine some of the fundamentals of our political faith.'[8]

How should this offensive be met? The greatest hope lay with the very forces that Heath sought to crush. The protest movements of the late sixties, the growth of militancy and the wave of direct action by workers in the fight for their rights, seemed to him to be the key to a process of rebirth of the democratic spirit of the nation, through which people would learn political responsibility in action, and by a process of peaceful but active protest, would impose change on the parliamentary leaders at the top:

'The best of our history has been change from below led by the Chartists, the Tolpuddle Martyrs, Mrs Pankhurst, the suffragette leaders, and hundreds of thousands of nameless people who stood up against authority, suffered and won. They gave us democracy – not the kings and queens.

None of these people were revolutionaries thirsting for blood. The British tradition of political change rests on countless individuals with obstinate consciences who would not put up with unfair laws and pushed until parliament changed them.

It's all happening again.

A great new movement for reform is building up – peaceful but determined and coming from below, and the leaders of it are tough and self-confident and irreverent.

Top people despise the public. No wonder the public despise them.

The so-called credibility problem is not that people don't trust individual politicians. It means they are learning from the shipworkers and the students and the miners and the women, the railwaymen and the dockers that if you want to get things changed you've got to do something about it yourself.

This is a rebirth of our national self-confidence.'[9]

Birth of a heresy

These views led him in a radically different direction from other Labour Party leaders – even those who agreed with him on matters of government policy. He established a remarkable new relationship with new layers of militants emerging within the working class movement and the other, new movements he supported.

He gave open, public support to the new rise of industrial militancy – almost unthinkable for a Labour politician in a situation where the Heath government sought to brand the unions as the main culprits for the nation's ills.

Wilson refused to endorse the UCS work-in on the grounds of its illegality. Benn, who had been directly involved in setting up UCS and its forerunner, headed the Glasgow support demonstration arm-in-arm with Communist shop stewards. In August 1972 he came out in full support of the five dockers jailed by the government and took a centre spread in the *Daily Mirror*, at editor Hugh Cudlipp's invitation, to put their case. 'According to the Prime Minister,' he said, 'Britain has been taken to the brink of anarchy because five dockers disobeyed the law.'

> 'If that was true the situation would be serious. But it is not true. No five men could undermine our country. What has really frightened the Cabinet is that millions of people who did *not* break the law expressed their sympathy and support for the dockers. One of them was me.'[10]

He backed the miners in 1972 and again in 1974. He dubbed the three-day week a National Lockout and set up, through the Labour Party, a special monitoring service to challenge Heath's claim that the closedowns were the result of a fuel shortage caused by the miners.

He became 'Mr Unions' in the Labour Party, and got promoted, by the establishment, to public enemy number one. Gone were the affectionate, if dismissive allusions to 'Hover Benn', the incompetent dreamer. The media fashioned a new image for him: power-mad Benn, the dangerous red. He was portrayed as stirring up anarchy, fomenting unrest to lay the basis of a socialist power grab. At best he was a dangerous lunatic and at worst an evil despot.

Behind these allegations lay a profound dilemma, with which he was trying to grapple in his assessment of the constitutional implications of Heath's attacks. How could the sovereignty of the people be reconciled with existing parliamentary methods and institutions?

This problem was to overshadow his political career, and indeed British politics, from this point on. In the 1972 Shadow Cabinet paper on 'Law and Order' which first laid these problems out, Benn argued that:

> 'Democracy and socialism in Britain are built upon three principles, which we have struggled to establish over the years, and which form the basis of consent on which our system of government rests.
>
> The first is the supremacy of conscience over law. The second is the accountability of power to the people. The third is the sovereignty of the people over parliament.
>
> These three principles are now under direct attack. The Tory campaign on law and order is designed to get us to accept the idea that all laws made by the state must be blindly obeyed . . . We are, therefore, confronted in Britain with the need to look again at the fundamentals of our system of politics and government.'[11]

But how was the sovereignty of the people over parliament, and the supremacy of conscience over law, to be expressed? Did the people, or even sectoral interests amongst the people – such as the unions – have the right to determine what should and should not be law, by means other than elections? Benn seemed to support the unions 'taking the law into their own hands'. But in challenging the rule of law, they were challenging the institutions of government.

When angry dockers confronted Sir John Donaldson and his Industrial Relations Court, when miners confronted the police for control of the streets, when UCS workers confronted the property laws of the land by taking over their factories, and when Clay Cross councillors disobeyed the government and refused to raise rents, they were not merely breaking the law but attempting to make it. By their stand they declared what, in their view, should take place in a just society. By implication they asked others not just to support them, but to join and even imitate them; and they declared to the government that an attempt to proceed with its law would render the country ungovernable.

They were telling parliament what laws it could not make – and by implication, what laws it should make. By the very nature of their confrontation they began to usurp the legislative function of parliament and undermine the authority of the state and the rule of the rich and privileged. Were they not therefore usurping parliamentary democracy? And by supporting their actions, was Benn not doing likewise?

The constitutional issues Benn had raised were not new. The power of the 'mob' has provoked a debate, dividing left from right, in most revolutions. And in the English Civil War – history's first popular struggle for the sovereignty of parliament – the conservative parliamentary faction had grown up around hostility to mobs of common people who sought to bend parliament to their will and against the king and church hierarchy, by means of petitions and demonstrations. The conservative Presbyterian MP Edward Waller had argued against conceding church reform to the mob on the following basis:

> 'I look upon the episcopacy as a counterscarp or outwork which, if it be taken by this assault of the people and, withal, this mystery be revealed 'that we must not deny them anything when they ask it thus in troops', we may, in the next place, have as hard a place to

> defend our property, as we have lately had to recover it from the Prerogative. If, by multiplying hands and petitions, they prevail for an equality in things ecclesiastical the next demand may perhaps be *lex Agraria*, the like equality in things temporal.'[12]

If this went on, he continued, we would have the same situation as in ancient Rome. When the people discovered the power of *legem rogare* – the ability to *ask* the Senate to make a law – they quickly proceeded to *legem ferre*, which was the right to make their own laws. But then, he argued, they set the Senate on one side and put in dictators to suit their pleasure.

Waller had enunciated the classical left-right division in European politics of the next four centuries, which was not initially an argument between socialism and capitalism, but between the *parties of order* and the *popular parties*. His arguments have been echoed down the centuries.

By championing inherent rights which could legitimately be defended against parliament, by deducing from this the sovereignty of the people over parliament, and above all by endorsing direct popular action, Benn seemed to have opened the door to revolution.

Yet he himself wanted to avoid a revolutionary overthrow of an elected government. This would result, he felt, in an 'authoritarian government of the right or the left'. He wanted to combine legislative change through parliament with popular protest in such a way that governments would still be changed by parliamentary elections.

He therefore established a distinction between 'revolutionary action to replace parliament' and 'law-breaking in pursuit of conscientious objection'.

The latter embodied the supremacy of conscience over law:

> 'That concept of law-breaking in pursuit of conscience rests on our belief that our prime duty is to each other. If this leads individuals into conflict with the law, these individuals must be ready to take the consequences non-violently. In our democracy no man should tell another man to break the law, nor should any man break the law to bypass parliament. But a person who is punished for breaking an unjust law may, if he is sincere and his cause wins public sympathy, create a public demand to have that unjust law changed through parliament.'[13]

He argued that the labour movement's traditions and respect for parliament would lead it to choose peaceful methods of change:

> 'Since the trade union movement believes itself, correctly, to have been a major founding force in parliamentary democracy through its support for the Chartists and others, it is not likely to reject its own history by seeking the overthrow of a government freely elected.'[14]

he explained in 1980.

Arguing the dockers' case he asserted in the *Mirror* article that:

> 'There isn't a Lenin lurking in the wings. The Angry Brigade couldn't pick up a hundred votes in any constituency. The thing that makes this country – with all its injustices and imperfections – such a law-abiding place is not the fact that we've got police and courts with judges in long wigs.
>
> It is that we are basically decent, generous, compassionate, hardworking and fairminded people. These qualities and not the statute book are our copper-bottomed guarantee against anarchy – so long as we play it fair amongst ourselves.'[15]

But was it true in practice that a parliamentary tradition and a non-violent tradition were one and the same thing? The miners, dockers and sit-in strikers had used considerable force, and frequently broke the law, despite their support for parliamentary democracy.

The problem lay in the *independence of the state* to which Benn had drawn attention when he analysed Heath's strategy. 'The Tory campaign on Law and Order is designed to get us to accept the idea that all laws are made by the state and must be blindly obeyed', he had said. Respect for parliament was not the same as respect for the state, although Heath wanted to use respect for parliament to impose respect for the state.

The establishment's hypocritical objections to 'outside interference in parliament' were not so much directed against the subversion of elections as against the subversion of unelected and unaccountable bodies such as the police, the courts, and the civil service.

Respect for parliamentary democracy was no guarantee against confrontations between union militants and these unelected bodies. By arguing that the state could not under all circumstances draw authority from parliamentary elections, Benn gave legitimacy to these confrontations.

Furthermore, when the government attempted to use the issue of 'law and order' to increase respect for the state, the result was the reverse of what it sought. It decreased the authority of the government instead of increasing that of the state. Union militants who had begun holding parliament in the greatest respect were firstly forced to confront the state in the shape of the police and the Industrial Relations Court, and then the government which was directing and inspiring the state's attack on them.

The establishment looked on with horror and saw, not controlled non-violence but lawlessness and mob force; not peaceful protest action but an open subversion of their state and its government. Behind the denunciation of Benn's 'Red Dictatorship' lay fear, not of Benn himself, but of the mob they saw behind him.

Thus was Benn converted from a dissident to a heretic. The new role was thrust on him, not chosen. His gospel was heretical because it offered a *morality subversive of the state*. Just as the gospel of Diggers and Levellers, during the English Civil War, had subverted an order based on the King's false claim to speak for God, so Benn challenged an order based on the prime minister's false claim to speak for the people.

The religious state of Charles I claimed to speak for God, but in reality spoke for the old aristocracy. The parliamentary state of Elizabeth II claimed to speak for the electorate, but in reality spoke for the capitalist class.

It was not relevant that the electorate exists and God does not. Neither were represented by those who claimed their authority. Benn threatened to cement the revolt of the working class with new parliamentary ideals, just as the old heretics cemented revolts against the nobility with new religious ideals.

But was he not doomed to a similar fate? They sought to reform God, and he, parliament. True, parliament was more accessible: but the problem confronted by his followers was not so much parliament as *those who spoke in its name*. What should be done about the state? Benn found himself in an ambiguous relation with the very forces who looked to him. Although he endorsed popular action, he sought to limit it, reading his own philosophy into workers' actions when their experiences moved them in a different direction. He counselled passive resistance to people who had no option, faced with police coercion or repression from the courts, but to respond with effective measures of self-defence – which meant using force and breaking the law. 'There are two ways forward', he said of UCS workers,

> 'One is to carry on working while it is legally possible and then shift the campaign on to a wider industrial and political front.
>
> The other is to choose the dead-end of a clash with the law. This has been clearly and rightly ruled out in all the statements made by the leaders of UCS.'[16]

But the work-in was already technically illegal, and the workforce had already risked a clash with the law. This clash did not take place, not because of the stewards' resolve to avoid it, but because the government prudently decided not to *invoke* the law, fearing that the justice of the UCS cause would inspire millions to support them against the existing legal system. Two visions of society clashed on the banks of the Clyde: two laws, two worlds, two classes. The government refused the battle because the workforce stood up for their law against the government's, and neither Benn's interpretation nor the stewards' reassurances could disguise this fact.

The more the establishment sought to strengthen its powers against occupations and pickets, and the more it sought to illegalise trade union activity, the more ambiguous Benn's approach became. Workers at Kirkby Manufacturing Enterprises in Liverpool, with whom he collaborated to set up a workers' co-op, began their occupation by barricading the gates and training fire-hoses on the entrance to use on police if entry were forced. This certainly risked confrontation with the law – yet without such measures the co-op would never have seen the light of day.

The issue was further complicated by the fact that Benn did not distinguish between *force* and *violence*, particularly destructive individual violence. The successes of the industrial movement of the early seventies lay in its ability to use weight of numbers, and popular support, to overawe the state. At the battle of Saltley Gate, the police gave up the attempt to remove a crucial picket because of the sheer numbers which joined it, and subsequent ruling class strategy centred on trying to limit numbers of pickets.

The nub of the ensuing debate, in which the trade union and Labour Party leaders sided with the establishment, was not trade union violence but *who had the right to use coercive force* – the state or the unions. Cutting down picket sizes removed from the unions the right to use force, thus making them ineffective.

Benn tended to identify the use of force with acts of individual terrorism such as 'bomb-throwing in Morecambe', constantly using analogies with the Angry Brigade, with black-bearded and bomb-throwing anarchists, and with hooliganism, to classify revolutionary activity – unconsciously adopting the very terms which the establishment used to criminalise trade union activity. The result was that he never fully confronted the problem of force in politics.

He infuriated the establishment by seeming to side-step their real objections – perhaps because they could not state their real objections. This came to a head with the miners' strike of 1974, of which Benn was almost the patron saint. This strike was not a revolutionary act, but it had revolutionary implications. In it the working class did something it had not done even in 1926. The miners challenged, not just the policies, but the *composition and existence* of a British government – by means of force.

In a sense they exercised, for a brief instant, the divine right to unseat governments which had until then been the prerogative of bankers, monarchs and Orangemen.

The establishment spent the years that followed trying to ensure that this right would never again be exercised. The first step, after Labour came to office in 1974, was to be the exorcism of Benn himself.

Unions and social change

These problems did not loom large during the Tory government's life, when concepts of passive resistance and active interference could coexist. But they did raise problems for future strategy. Benn's approach had been born under conditions of defensive struggle. How should the labour movement proceed when it wanted to go on the offensive – particularly when in government? How could it secure positive social change, in the teeth of the resistance encountered by the 1964-69 government?

Benn again seemed in a contradiction. He explained clearly that change would be thwarted by agencies *not* subject to control by the Commons. Yet they could not be confronted and defeated *except* by parliament. Some method was therefore needed whereby parliament and people could act together to defeat them. Benn wanted to avoid violence or unconstitutional action, but wanted also to offer a popular challenge to 'unaccountable centres of power'.

His answer was to build into his strategy the one source of legitimate, extra-state force which was sanctioned – albeit grudgingly – by the constitution: industrial action and bargaining. He proposed a radical change in trade union strategy. The unions should *reverse their traditional relation to the Labour Party and use their industrial power to secure social change*. He argued in 1971:

> 'The trade union movement – in both the private and the public sector – ought now to develop a conscious long-term policy of negotiating itself into a position of real power in industry . . . If the trade union movement were to bargain as strongly for industrial power as it does for higher wages then management would also be ready to concede. Because then the alternative would be the high financial cost of a strike or the relatively low cost of sharing their power with the workers in their own firm. No-one could expect to achieve everything in the first year. But if the trade union movement set itself the target of negotiating for the workers power in each firm to acquire greater control of that firm, by agreement with the present management, over a five-year period – in my opinion it would succeed.'[17]

This ambitious project demanded a new alliance, on a different foundation, between unions and party. Benn was breaking with the long-standing tradition which saw the unions as dealing with questions of working conditions in the factory, and the Labour Party as dealing with political issues through parliament and local councils.

The first step was to unite the unions and the party around a common set of policies. Assessing how to respond to Heath's offensive, he wrote in his Shadow Cabinet paper:

> '. . . if the unions, and the party, are to face an election campaign on the issues which the Cabinet would like to make central, unity between the whole labour movement has got to be complete.

> We have got to think in terms of a joint programme covering a complete range of policies, discussed and agreed between us, and on which we can fight together for public support to form the basis upon which the next Labour government will work.'[18]

But this involved a new role for the unions, in which they ceased to be a purely defensive force and began to serve as a responsible force for social change. In short, they had to become politically active.

> 'The mere defeat of this government and the election of another Labour government will not therefore, of itself, transform our society overnight, or automatically into a fair, democratic and humane community . . . The last Labour government – in which I was proud to serve – faced and surmounted appalling economic difficulties and carried through a formidable programme of socialist reforms.
>
> It also made some mistakes. One of those mistakes was in our approach to industrial relations, and we lost the confidence of many of our own people . . . [but] it is simply not good enough to blame the Labour government or the parliamentary Labour Party entirely for our defeat in 1970. The trade union movement, with all its virtues, must also accept its share of responsibility . . . You have allowed yourselves to be presented to the public as if you actively favoured the conservative philosophy of personal acquisitiveness.
>
> The fact that the trade union movement came into being to fight for social justice, as well as higher wages, has just not got across . . . neither the party nor the TUC has given sufficient support to other movements of legitimate protest and reform led by women, by the old, and by the young and others – who are, in reality, engaged in our common struggle.'[19]

This defensive attitude on the part of the unions, however, was also the fault of the restrictions which society placed on them:

> 'One of the reasons why wage militancy has tended to be the peg around which trade unions have concentrated is that it is the one area, indeed the only area, where trade unions have been permitted by law to be effective. If you say to the trade union movement, as we still do 'the law does not entitle you to discuss investment, the prices of your products, research and development, export marketing, product development', then the whole weight of trade union activity will remain concentrated on the wages side and this may not be effective in securing a real change in the balance of wealth and power in society.'[20]

In pursuit of this conviction, Benn embarked on a tireless round of meetings and discussions with trade unionists at every level. But his project did not have implications for the unions alone. At the same time that he began his rise to popularity with the stewards' movement and the left trade union leaders, he began to emerge as a new champion of the Labour Party left. He was becoming a new phenomenon in British politics: a left wing Labour MP with an active base in the unions.

His influence in the party grew steadily. He was appointed Shadow Secretary for Trade and Industry. He became chairman of the party. He collaborated with a rising layer of backroom intellectual 'Young Turks' who stimulated thought about new directions for the party – notably Stuart Holland, who put together a formidable case for government intervention in industry. He served on the NEC's Information Committee, its Home Policy Committee (which drafted its new programme) and its Human Rights, Science and Education, and Transport Committees.

Most important for him, however, was the work on industrial policy. As chairman of the NEC's Industrial Policy Committee in 1972-73, as Shadow Secretary for Trade and Industry, and through his links with the stewards' movement and bodies like the Institute for Workers' Control, he served as a channel for the formulation of new policy ideas and their discussion in both the party and the unions.

The most crucial document to arise from this period was the 'Green Paper' produced by the Industrial Policy Committee. Entitled *The National Enterprise Board: Labour's State Holding Company*, it became a point of reference for the left in the party.

The argument behind the document was that successive governments, using Keynesian demand management techniques, had been unable to keep control of the economy because they could not direct investment. The government and unions had to be directly involved in the decision-making process, particularly about major investments, which companies until now had seen as the prerogative of higher management.

There were three prongs to this strategy. First, Labour would expand state ownership, if necessary through compulsory acquisition, so that it could exercise direct influence in important sectors of the economy. Stuart Holland felt it was particularly important to control one or two leading firms in each department of what he called the 'meso-economic' sector: firms which were so large that they were able to manipulate the market by controlling supply, evading price competition. He argued that ownership of twenty-five leading firms would give the government decisive influence. Significantly this proposal was excluded by Wilson's veto from the 1973 Manifesto.

Second, the government would enter into 'planning agreements' with a much wider range of firms. The government would get together with management and with unions and discuss the firm's investment proposals. In accordance with objectives determined by its own overall plans, and by social need, it would try to ensure that the companies' plans were altered so that the government's economic objectives could be met. Firms that went along with this would be rewarded by the government 'playing ball' with them in terms of grants, commercial information, contracts, and so on.

Finally, the government would also involve the workforce directly, through these tripartite discussions, in formulating both its own policy and the firm's. It would involve them in carrying out these decisions too. Decision-making would be shared and decentralised, making the whole process more democratic.

The state holding company would make this possible. It would centralise the information, expertise and money that the government commanded, giving it an overall view of the economy which no individual firm possessed. The government could use this relative advantage, and its ownership of key industries, to make companies play along with it.

Benn argued that taxpayers were putting millions into industry through grants and subsidies, and had a right to know how it was used and even to control its use.

As he expected from his 1968 clash with Keith Joseph and Callaghan, he encountered a powerful lobby inside and outside the Labour Party, which objected to the government playing such a direct role.

Clause Four, the Bevan tradition, and workers' control

The discussion forced him to return to the debates of the sixties from which he had stood aside in the past, concerning Clause Four of the party constitution and its commitment to public ownership.

It was at this point that the first difference in approach, later to lead to an open breach, emerged between Benn and the old Tribunite/Bevanite school of socialism.

The intellectual work of Tony Crosland in the fifties had laid the basis for the view that the ideals of socialism could be realised within a permanently mixed economy. Crosland argued that Keynesian state intervention – government spending to prop up the economy by managing demand for goods – was a link between the party's socialist ideals and governing a mixed economy.

Gaitskell, as party leader in the late fifties and early sixties, had taken this through to its logical conclusion. Before he died in 1963, he had embroiled the party in a bitter fight over his attempt to remove the commitment, contained in Clause Four, to the *eventual* public ownership of the *whole* economy. He had argued that a narrow and doctrinaire commitment to outdated ideas prevented it reaching a wider audience of middle class voters.

Labour should come forward, he argued, as the inventor of the policies the Tories were now applying, but with the added bonus of socialist morality, concern for the weak and needy, a striving to replace outdated class privilege with broad social benefits for all, an end to 'Colonel Blimp' warlike posturing abroad, and a broad multi-class appeal.

In spite of the fact that there was little practical difference between what Gaitskell proposed and what the party had already done, the controversy over Clause Four stirred up tremendous antagonisms. Gaitskell was, in effect, saying that Labour should no longer be a socialist party. This implied it should no longer be a working class party.

In practice, Labour had not been socialist. But many who considered themselves socialist worked within it, and supported it, because they could accept state nationalisation and state intervention, however slowly applied, as part of a gradual process of *transition* to socialism, reflecting the party's class commitment. The traditional, Bevanite view was that socialism would be won through parliament by buying the economy from the capitalists, piece by piece, until it was all state-owned, and therefore all socialist.

This was one reason that Bevan's successors could work within unified parliamentary teams with the party right wing. They felt that every extension of the state sector, and every extension of social justice won through the state, was a step in humanity's forward march.

The great value and great limitation of this idea was that it saw every piece of parliamentary legislation as a tiny move in the great never-ending forward shuffle of the British people. On the one hand this inspired the labour movement to feats of great endurance under adversity, in the belief that history was *eventually* on its side. But when the postwar consensus drew to an end and the gains of 1945 began to be withdrawn, the Bevanites could not accept that the obstacle to progress was in fact their chosen instrument – the British Tory state. They lowered their sights while Benn raised his.

More serious still was the fact that the traditional unity of the labour movement was built around electoral advance. As the electoral road became stonier this unity came under greater and greater stress.

Thus the policies of the 1964 government had in reality been Gaitskellite, although Wilson was elected as a candidate of the left. Benn felt that the experience of this government proved such policies could no longer be applied because the postwar consensus, which permitted them, was dissolving. Looking back on his time in this government ten years later, he explained that:

> 'the thing which has made me so convinced that you can't have this so-called centre party or Tory 'wet' solution or right-wing solution is that I tried to run it for years, from 1964 to 1968, when I began to see what was really happening.
>
> I was part of the policy which is now presented as being so brand-new by the Social Democrats, who are really resuscitating a policy that I worked harder on than anyone else, and I can tell you from experience [that it] fails, is undemocratic, and widens the gap between rich and poor.
>
> The policy was to use the state to make capitalism work. To pour in public money to private industry, to merge companies together, to do deals with businessmen, and so on, and the more I looked at it, the more I realised that it really was a corporate state we were making. We tried to get businessmen, bankers and maybe a few top trade union leaders in with ministers, sort it all out and keep

> people who created the wealth out entirely. And it wasn't efficient, it didn't improve our rate of growth, it wasn't egalitarian, it wasn't democratic, it was very secretive and it was accompanied by a steady and continuing decline of British industry. That is why I should never go back to that again and that is what made me think about democracy and socialism.'[21]

Benn summarised his alternative in the rallying call which was adopted as the goal of the 1973 manifesto: for a 'fundamental and irreversible shift in the balance of power and wealth in favour of working people and their families'.

The reforms carried out by the next government would so alter the organisation of society, and the accepted rights and responsibilities of its various sectors, that it would permanently weaken the capitalist class, and permanently strengthen the working class. It would establish gains which, like the right to vote, the right to free trade unions and the welfare state itself, would become so much a part of the British way of life that they could not be taken away again.

What were these new gains to be? For Benn, the decisive advance was the *public accountability of industry*. This was his version of Clause Four, his vision of the goal of socialist policy. The necessary alliance between parliament and people meant that a pincer approach to public accountability was called for. On the one hand the government itself had to become directly involved in decision-making in industry. Above all, investment decisions had to be taken in consultation with government and, if necessary, vetoed by it. On the other hand, workers themselves, in the firms concerned, had to be drawn into this process.

The 'industrial franchise', as Benn dubbed it, was vital. It was his answer both to the control of private industry *and* to the bureaucratic nature of nationalised industry. He could thus refute a biting and popular Tory anti-socialist jibe, that state control restricted individual freedom. Labour was committed to using the Tory state, and could not make the marxist rejoinder that if state control proved bureaucratic, the answer might be a truly democratic state. Benn could now counter this objection by calling for the transfer of powers from the state to working people.

He saw this in the same light as the democratisation of society at large. Just as people were alienated from political decision-making by the haughty and arrogant conduct of top politicians, so they were alienated at work by the control exercised over their lives by huge, unaccountable and faceless corporations.

> 'Today a wide gap has opened up between man as a citizen enjoying full civil rights, enjoying greater freedom to think and move and act according to his wishes, and man as a wage-earner who at his place of work enjoys few of these gifts.
>
> When a man enters the factory gates in the morning, he sheds much of his dignity with his overcoat, leaving both on a peg in the locker room. In the workshop he is part of an authoritarian type of society which differs sharply from his normal existence.'[22]

Since the faceless corporations now exercised as much power as governments and maybe more, they too should be brought under popular control. But this could not just be done via central government. This ran the risk of reproducing within the nationalised industries the very corporate structure of faceless power which prevailed in the political system as a whole. Therefore, in both public and private industry, decision-making would have to be shared, and workers brought in and given the right to a direct say in the running of the industries where they worked:

> 'The substitution of Lord Robens for a bunch of private coal owners is not the same as socialism. Nationalisation does not, of itself, shift the balance of power in society, democratise industry, nor entrench new values in work . . . common ownership is only, at best, a mere instrument or technique to be judged by a political test. The central question that remains to be settled is therefore the democratisation of public enterprise from the bottom up.'[23]

But this was what defined the special, new role of the unions. They were to struggle at the workplace, to determine how their firm was run.

> 'If we are going to talk about industrial policy let us start with the people. Let's forget about legislation for a moment and start talking about industrial democracy . . . democracy means that the people ultimately control their managers. Just that, no more and no less. It's time we asked ourselves some fundamental questions about the management of industry.
>
> For example, why should the people who own a firm control it? We abandoned that principle years ago in the political arena.

For centuries the people who owned the land in Britain ran parliament. It took a hundred years of struggle to give people the power to choose and remove their political managers – MPs and ministers. If we can trust the country to democracy why on earth can't we trust individual firms to the people who work in them?

This is not a particularly revolutionary doctrine in all conscience. No-one is suggesting – at least I am not – that you do it by throwing petrol bombs or starting a guerilla movement in Morecambe. You could do it just as easily by peaceful industrial bargaining and by removing the obstacles to it by legislation.'[24]

This, to Benn, was the political significance of planning agreements. They were not merely an instrument of state control, but also of popular democracy. 'The whole purpose of the planning agreement', he said, 'is to introduce that democratic tripartite element into industrial policy . . .'

'That is the unique contribution that the shop floor and the labour movement made in the development of policy in our years of opposition. There must be open disclosure; there must be democratic planning . . . I think that the development of a three-way relationship between the government, the trade union movement and management – I am talking about professional management – even in the nationalised industries, does contain within it an ingredient absolutely lacking in old Labour thinking.'[25]

What role did this assign to industry's traditional vested interests – the shareholders, directors, and managers? It would not eliminate the investors, or even profit and competition. 'We are not a party of confiscation', he explained to the 1973 conference, opposing a *Militant* resolution calling for widespread nationalisation with minimal compensation. He sought methods to erode the powers of the owners of capital without eliminating them. '. . . investors there will always be', he said, discussing Clause Four,

'but there is no valid reason why the investors' money should give them first claim to control, before those who invest their lives. Political democracy wrested the control of parliament from those who owned the lands and the factories, and industrial democracy is a logical and necessary development of it.'[26]

He held, however, that professional management would not necessarily attach itself to the coat-tails of the shareholders, and that in the context of tripartite democracy they could be made to side with workers and government against the owners in the case of a clash.

Many critics saw this as milder than the Bevanites' ideas. Scargill quotes a memo from Arnold Weinstock in which he says that Benn's ideas could be used to increase profits, if it helped employees to accept the firm's objectives.[27]

But worker control had in other countries been as subversive of private property as nationalisation – and nationalisation, conversely, had not exactly ushered in the socialist commonwealth. The problem in each case was whether the aim was to reach a new compromise with the old owners, or to overcome their obstruction.

Establishment reaction to Benn was not based on what he proposed as such, but on the moral foundations he gave for actions to which workers were being driven. If investors did not have first claim to control, then why should they have any at all? If workers could assert their rights against investors' rights, what was wrong with factory seizures?

Both classes in Britain were watching Chile. Allende had reinstated a law, dating from 1933, which gave workers the right to demand state intervention against employers who transgressed their rights or the public interest. This law had lain unused on the statute books for forty years. But now it served as the excuse for the occupation, by 1973, of more than half the factories, with popular and factory committees bidding for control of the whole economy. In mid-1972 the Minister for the Economy, Pedro Vuscovic, drew the very conclusion which the establishments of Chile and Britain alike most feared – that the only solution to the problems of the economy was to hand it over to these committees.[28]

Was this a danger in Britain? It was lessened, but not eliminated, by the fact that Benn himself didn't want to get rid of the investors. Indeed, the idea of planning agreements itself seemed to conflict with democracy. Why should workers only get a minority one-third share in control?

A further third would be government representatives. Since the government itself would be a Labour government, tripartite control would in Benn's view effectively give workers a two-thirds majority.

This would work if the government was represented by agents loyal to it and to working people. But what if the government was represented by a hostile state? Workers might react in one of two ways: by conceding to imposed agreements against their interests, or by resorting to industrial action, not just against their employers but against the state itself, deploying on the streets and at the factory gates the numbers denied access to the boardroom. But the government could now take one of two steps. It could weigh in on the side of the workers – or it could weigh in on the side of the state. Benn's policies thus guaranteed that the Industry Department in 1974-75 would become the cockpit of a momentous struggle between contending classes, in which no less than the authority and legality of the state would be at stake. Pressure would indeed grow to give legal authority to the actions and organisations thrown up by the struggle, by open-ended government backing for workers' occupations.

Such moves would have undermined the combined foundation of state and property, by suggesting a different type of state, under popular control, in which all citizens had the right to take part. This was the kind of state which Marx had discerned in the Paris Commune, and which Lenin had wanted to use as the foundation of Russian democracy. But Russian soviet democracy, already sapped by civil war, was ultimately usurped by Stalin's bureaucracy, giving rise to a fear that all socialist experiments would end up thus. History had not yet proved whether this fear was correct or not. But in the West, the evidence so far had blunted the urge to revolution.

Here was a danger that as Western democracy declined, Marx's old ideal could be revived in the fire of struggle – lit by the spark of Benn's ideas. With occupations averaging one a fortnight, it was hardly surprising that his ideas disturbed the employers.

It can be seen that these ideas were far removed from orthodox Labour left thinking. For most *Tribune* members, workers' control was an amendment which *Militant* supporters added to nationalisation motions. Above all Benn had a different – though also reformist – concept of *transition* to socialism. He did not see socialism coming from the slow conquest of ownership in order to get control. He saw it coming from the slow conquest of control in order to get ownership.

But in 1973 Benn's ideas could co-exist with both Wilson's and the more left-wing Tribunites', for they had not been tested in practice. Unity was forged in the party around policies that meant three different things to three different groups of people. For Wilson and his acolytes, their eyes on office, the new policies were no more than public declarations of faith, rather than a real statement of intent. For those who still held to the *Tribune* gospel they represented a new way of stating the old policies of slow nationalisation and Keynesian state intervention. For Benn, for a small number of activists around him in the party, and for tens of thousands of militant shop stewards, they represented a new relation between government and people in which workers would at long last play an active role in shaping and determining their own future.

The whole Labour Party therefore rallied around a radical common programme with the adoption, in 1973, of *Labour's Programme for Britain*, the most left wing programme since 1945. The test of Labour's new-found unity, and Benn's place within it, was not long in coming. Within three months the Tory government collapsed before the onslaught of the miners, and the 1973 manifesto became the election manifesto of Benn's second Labour government.

3. The Enemy Within

> It must at least be conceded that the Liberal Party showed ten times more courage in the '80s and '90s and again immediately before the war, than the English Labour Party, which is in the same miserable reformist position, has ever shown. Gladstone challenged the whole system over Home Rule. In 1911 the Liberal Party broke for ever the power of the House of Lords . . . during the Home Rule controversy, Liberal leaders were actually cut at society dinner-parties. The Labour leaders have never done anything to occasion such a rebuff.
>
> Stephen Spender, *Forward from Liberalism*

The general election of February 1974 made Labour the largest party in the House of Commons, but without an overall majority. Six months later Wilson called fresh elections, and Labour won a further twenty seats from the Tories to secure a small overall majority.

The results confirmed Benn's views that left wing policies were no obstacle to success with the voters. Yet Labour's share of the vote, at 37.1 per cent, was almost unchanged when, five years later, it lost to Thatcher. Behind Labour's 1974 triumph lay a devastating defeat for the Tories.

Their vote fell from 13 million in 1970 to 10 million in October 1974. At 35.9 per cent, this was the lowest share they had got since 1906. Their unionist voting base in Northern Ireland had gone to the Ulster Loyalists. The Liberals, with six million votes, were only prevented from becoming a much larger force in the Commons by the 'first past the post' voting system.

The Scottish and Welsh nationalist parties probably took as much from Labour as from the Tories. But this disguised the real political impact of their advance, which was to turn the Tory Party outside England into a fringe group. The October election further reinforced the division of England into Tory shires and Labour cities. There were fewer big city Tory MPs than in living memory. This fragmentation of the Tories' base hammered home the message of the miners' strike: they could not govern.

Labour came to office, as Benn had hoped, with a mandate for radical change, with the opposition in total disarray, and with the active support of the unions. Benn entered the new government at the peak of his influence. He had already served four years as Shadow Secretary for Trade and Industry, and went straight into the crucial Cabinet post of Secretary of State for Trade and Industry. He was in a first class position to set about implementing Labour's industrial strategy, the centrepiece of the manifesto; and the labour movement seemed in an excellent position to carry through a programme of radical social transformation.

The outcome was an unqualified disaster. In late 1974 a world slump, the first since the thirties, hit the Western industrial world. The British economy passed through a series of protracted crises, beginning with a violent surge of inflation – at one stage reaching a year-on-year rate of over 30 per cent – and followed by continual balance of payments problems culminating in the sterling crisis of 1976. Sterling was baled out only at the cost of a near total reversal of social policy, dictated by the International Monetary Fund.

Benn's own policies got short shrift. The Industry Act was neutered, and Labour's industrial democracy proposals turned into participation schemes which helped management more than the shop floor. The British people voted two to one in favour of Common Market entry in the referendum which he had brought about; and the defeat served as the occasion for his dismissal from the Department of Trade and Industry and relegation to the Energy Department.

Between 1975 and 1978 public spending on the social services fell in real terms by 17 per cent and capital spending by nearly half. Labour took office with unemployment at half a million, and left with one and a quarter million officially seeking work. In 1974 there were 1,140,000 people on the poverty line. By 1976 there were 2,280,000. Real disposable income fell, on average, by eight per cent between 1975 and 1979.[1]

Wilson's government had come to office committed to take

over where Attlee's 1945 government had left off. Instead it had started the destruction of most of Attlee's achievements.

What went wrong?

Democracy: second encounter

In contrast to 1964, there was no doubt this time that the capitalist class did not want Labour in office. Establishment reaction followed the grand old tradition of the lady in Claridges who remarked, just after the 1945 election,

> 'But this is terrible. They have elected a Labour government and the country will never stand for that.'[2]

Labour's manifesto was not acceptable to the wealthy. Business, banking and commerce launched a successful campaign, of unparalleled ferocity, to change the government and its course.

Benn expected a counter-offensive. But he entered office at least outwardly confident that it could be rebuffed.

'Do the British people really want a society in which industrialists and bankers have more power over Britain's economic future than the governments they elect?' he had asked in his speech to the *Financial Times* June 1973 conference.

> 'As the debate . . . develops we shall see big business come out of its corner and start fighting in earnest against these policies. And when that happens the whole campaign will be rather different from the campaign of Mr Cube a generation ago. People will not be quite so ready to fall for that old line, now that they know a bit more about the ugly face of capitalism . . . No wonder the Prime Minister wishes that that argument had not started. That may be why he is trying to shift it back to the safer ground of an imaginary leadership crisis within the Labour Party. I doubt if he will succeed.'[3]

Yet the last paragraph above shows how ill-prepared Benn was for the form which the offensive took. The 'imaginary' leadership crisis in the party became the decisive lever of establishment strategy. In their hour of need the capitalists turned, not just to the Lords, to Whitehall, to the International Monetary Fund (IMF) and the Confederation of British Industry (CBI), but to the leadership of the party and unions. They found the support they were looking for. Benn was facing a war on two fronts: inside, and outside, the labour movement.

Why was he the target? Although few capitalists wanted Labour in office, the miners' strike had given them no choice. Divided and fearful, they could not unseat the government, and so had to subvert it. But few wanted to subvert the institution of parliament itself, on which state authority rested. It was best that parliament should itself be the apparent instrument for the defeat of Labour's programme—and hence its left wing.

Benn was an obvious obstacle to this because his views, and his alone, could give legitimacy to any active working class resistance to such a manoeuvre. The attack therefore unfolded in three stages. First, Benn and his industrial policies were exorcised. Then the parliamentary left was isolated and silenced in parliament, in the wake of the EEC referendum. Finally, the economic crisis was brought to bear on the government – in the usual form of a sterling crisis – in such a manner that it could be forced to 'see sense' and abandon its remaining socialistic follies to defend the pound.

Benn thus found himself under fire from his first days in office. He had to translate Labour's manifesto commitments into legislative proposals. Working from the 1973 Green Paper on Industrial Strategy he aimed to prepare an Industry Act establishing a National Enterprise Board with enough money and powers to serve as the main vehicle of Labour's industrial strategy.

At the same time he faced a series of calls to save jobs in collapsing industries and factories – ironically enough using powers of intervention bequeathed him by the Tories. The urgency was underlined by occupations at Triumph's Meriden motorcycle factory and the Kirkby Manufacturing Enterprises (KME) plant in Liverpool.

Two battle fronts soon defined themselves. From the business community there was unremitting hostility, spearheaded by the CBI and aided by all the resources its money could command – advertising, the press, and powerful organised lobbies. In the Cabinet, as one of only five left wing Cabinet ministers (Benn, Castle, Foot, Shore and Silkin) Benn found himself under constant attack from Wilson and the Labour right, who held a Cabinet majority, and with whom the business community soon established a framework of common understanding.

Wilson had given lukewarm, but clear support to many of the Industrial Strategy's objectives at the 1973 party conference. He said:

> 'I must emphasise that the role of the National Enterprise Board is not just confined to the duties of a public holding and management agency . . . It will also act as a means to a further substantial expansion of public ownership through its power to take a controlling interest in relevant companies in profitable manufacturing industries.'[4]

Whether his declaration of support was based on belief or expediency, he opposed these policies in practice from the moment they became an issue of public contention. When the Green Paper was published in April 1973, media attacks centred on the public ownership proposals. His public opposition was featured under banner headlines such as WILSON NO TO STATE GRAB.

The NEC adopted the Green Paper proposals by a narrow seven to six majority, but in the manifesto the commitment was not spelt out and there were no clear indications as to the size and financing of the NEB. Giving evidence to the *Workers' Enquiry into the Labour Government's Industrial Policy* in 1980, Benn explained the result:

> 'The majority of the Cabinet did not understand or support the policies on which we were elected. It would be absurd to say that they did. Harold Wilson certainly had the idea that the NEB would be another IRC [Industrial Reorganisation Corporation] and virtually said so. Therefore the first problem was that although we had the support of conference and through the manifesto the electorate, we did not at any stage have the support of the Cabinet for the manifesto's industrial policies. This became clear when we put our Green Paper to the Cabinet subcommittee and the paper was rewritten with the crucial elements of our policy (as spelt out in the earlier report) left out.'[5]

It became clear that Wilson saw the overriding priority as the confidence of industry. He went to extraordinary lengths to get it. Terry Coleman of the *Guardian* gave one example of this, reporting a 1976 interview with Wilson:

> 'He said a sub-committee of a sub-committee of the executive [of the Labour Party] proposed to nationalise certain insurance companies. Now, I might think this was cynical, but he . . . dictated

> a letter first to himself and then a reply from himself. He sent both to the insurance people saying that they might like to send him his own letter and that his reply would then be published to show that the proposal was not government policy. A few months later he did the same thing with the merchant banks.'[6]

The Cabinet's right wing majority, led by Wilson, thus established a dialogue with industry and finance whose framework was the 'confidence of industry'. 'The restoration of "confidence" is described as if it had some objective reality', said Benn bitterly, 'whereas in truth "confidence" is nothing more than a political prize awarded by the world's bankers'.[7]

Industry and world banking now had a direct line of influence over Cabinet policy. All they needed to do, to thwart a policy they found objectionable, was succumb to a sudden crisis of confidence.

If this didn't work, the CBI was perfectly ready for plain disobedience. As Brian Sedgemore MP testified, the CBI's representative informed the Commons Industry Bill Standing Committee, point blank, that the CBI's members would refuse to abide by any information disclosure clauses in the new Act. 'We put it to him,' Sedgemore relates, 'that wasn't this tantamount to breaking the law? He replied, "Well, it's human nature that if you try to make people do things they don't do them".'[8]

None of the objections to the 'unconstitutional', 'illegal' or 'extraparliamentary' influence of the unions seemed to apply to the CBI. On the contrary, Wilson attacked as 'unrealistic' all those policy options which did *not* take into account the CBI's positions.

But as Benn explained to the *Workers' Enquiry*, Wilson did not have it easy. He had a Cabinet majority, but Benn's views were supported by the party activists and many of the unions. Wilson could not eliminate Benn's influence from the Cabinet, nor be confident of the loyalty of the Parliamentary Labour Party or unions, until the political climate had changed in his favour.

He realised his aims, therefore, through a further extension of Prime Ministerial powers, deepening a trend which he had initiated in 1964. 'Harold Wilson', said Benn later on, 'who formed four separate administrations over an eight year period,

> appointed or reshuffled 100 Cabinet ministers and 403 ministers of state and junior ministers, created 243 peers, appointed 24 chairmen

> of nationalised industries controlling 20 per cent of the nation's gross production and 16 chairmen of Royal Commissions to administer various policies or make recommendations for future policy, controlled all top line appointments within the civil service and of course, the honours list . . . The premiership in Britain is, in effect, an elected monarchy.'[9]

Benn saw this extension of Prime Ministerial powers as erecting yet another centre of unaccountable power, and as one of the most serious threats to democracy yet.

Whitehall's way

But these executive powers could not have been used in favour of business interests unless the administrative arm of the state – the civil service and above all Whitehall – had been prepared to go along with what was being done. And indeed, Whitehall did not merely go along with it, but inspired and guided it. This separate, non-elected centre of institutional power, created in its modern form by Gladstone in parallel with the very reforms that opened the age of universal suffrage, proved to be the crucial obstacle to the exercise of popular sovereignty through parliament. In theory the Commons was the first chamber of parliament and the Lords the second. In practice Whitehall was the first chamber, joined to the Commons by the Cabinet. It was the combination of Cabinet and Whitehall government against which Benn now found himself pitted.

The detailed execution of government policy was the responsibility of an army of trained administrators who, in theory, were impartial servants of the people. In practice the reverse was the case. Whitehall not only supported Wilson and the Labour right, but actively propagated and organised itself around the policies of the banking and business community, and consciously sabotaged Benn and his projects. The top civil servants effectively served as a 'government within a government', committed to ideals of continuity which in practice defended entrenched interests, divorced from the lives of ordinary people, and most important of all, accountable to no-one but the Prime Minister.

'In recent years', said Benn in 1979, in a lecture which was to have been given at Bristol University but was banned by the vice-chancellor, 'the power, role, influence and authority of the senior levels of the civil service in Britain have grown to such an extent as to create the embryo of a corporate state'.[10]

The tone was set in Benn's first encounter with his permanent secretary, Sir Anthony Part, an ex-army intelligence officer, later to become a director of Debenhams, EMI, the Life Association of Scotland, Metal Box, Savoy Hotels and even Lucas Aerospace, a firm with whose workers he dealt extensively from the Department of Trade and Industry. Sir Anthony greeted Benn with the immortal words, 'I presume, Secretary of State, that you don't intend to implement the industry proposals in Labour's manifesto'.

Benn pressed ahead; and top officials refused to co-operate in drawing up the 1974 White Paper on industrial policy, on the grounds that it was 'political'. In an article describing how the industrial strategy was defeated, Tom Forester explains that:

> 'The civil service was totally opposed to the interventionist strategy. Adrian Ham, who was Healey's special assistant, says there was a "Whitehall-wide conspiracy to stop Benn doing anything". This conspiracy included government ministers as well as the permanent secretaries, who meet regularly in their own unofficial inner Cabinet. "Some senior civil servants went so far as to brief anti-Benn ministers behind the backs of their own ministers", he says. "They had this obsession about defeating "Bennery" – a term coined in Whitehall long before Fleet Street picked it up." Ham says – as have others who were closely involved – that senior officials from the Department of Industry itself regularly briefed the Treasury on Benn's plans – the Treasury being the hub of opposition.'[11]

This opposition went well beyond attempts to influence the DTI's legislative proposals. When Benn began work on bailing out failing companies, and helping to establish the new worker-co-ops at Meriden, KME and the Scottish Daily News, the attitude of the civil service amounted to downright sabotage. According to Benn, their ingrained attitudes and habits of thought meant that they simply could not understand the proposals or the reasoning behind them. Beyond this, the structure of the service with its hierarchic and status-ridden career ladder, its basic class connections and mentality, and its constitutional role of offering continuity and defence of the status quo in government, gave it a natural sympathy with the business community and a natural antipathy to the working class.

Benn's officials could not understand the trail of stewards and other trades unionists who began to beat a path to his door. They saw this as unwarranted interference in government and even as an act of coercion. These ingrained attitudes determined the approach taken by Benn's administrators to the emerging co-ops.

KME workers were forced to enter a prolonged discussion about their constitution, which was eventually foisted on them by the Department before funding would be considered. The enterprise was in any case ludicrously underfunded. The original workers' proposal of £6.5 million was cut to £3.9 million, of which nearly £2 million simply paid off the former owners for the service of having closed the factory.

'By creating this figure the civil service had put a time and date on the collapse of the new venture', the convenor, Jack Spriggs, told the *Workers' Enquiry*. He also points out that the co-op's rules, as laid down by the civil service, 'left us with more restrictions than any other company within the public or private sector'. The co-op was not allowed to borrow from any other source, could not incur debts other than commercial debts, could not merge or associate with any other organisation, and finally the government had to declare in the House of Commons that the grant was never to be repeated.

Meriden workers fared no better. The civil service pulled out all the stops to prevent funds going to it. Benn declared, in the *Sunday Times* (6 July 1978), that the battle was fought 'with a fierceness and passion the like of which I have never come across in ministerial life'.

> 'Everything was brought to bear. The Industrial Advisory Board [which vets all major applications for funds and on which sit industrialists, bankers and trade union leaders] rejected Meriden's application more or less outright. The Department of Industry, the Cabinet and the Prime Minister's Offices each referred the issue to the Central Policy Review Staff, which gave a critical and pessimistic report. Finally, the Treasury, the most powerful office of all in Whitehall when it comes to providing funds, opposed the plan.'[12]

When money finally came it took the shape of a £4.2 million loan plus a £470,000 grant, of which £3.9 million had to be paid over to the owners and £200,000 to the government for its accountancy services.

In summary, the background to the struggle over the new Industry Act was very different to that for which Benn had hoped. He had counted on a united labour movement, whose parliamentary arm, by mobilising the moral support of the unions and their rank and file, would impose labour's manifesto on the unaccountable centres of power in the business community, Whitehall, and elsewhere.

Instead he found these centres of power united against the manifesto, together with a new centre of unaccountable power: Labour's Prime Minister and the majority of the Labour Cabinet, fired up and co-ordinated by Whitehall.

The powers of the Commons were being usurped, not just by extra-parliamentary forces, but by a section of parliament itself – the Cabinet – which was in theory accountable to the electorate and Commons, but in practice worked independently of it. This was the inevitable result of trying to continue with the implementation of consensus politics. As far as Benn was concerned it could only lead in one direction: towards a corporate state.

Benn now had to decide, not only how the labour movement could deal with its enemies outside its ranks, but how it could call to account its own leader, its own Cabinet, its own MPs, and its own union leaders. But not until the government had completed its disastrous term of office did he begin to come up with fresh answers. Meanwhile it took little more than fourteen months to turn the tide against him.

In early May 1974, the papers were reporting a public warning from Sir Michael Clapham, president of the CBI, against the 'interventionist line' of the government. A CBI delegation went to see Benn to check out warning signals they had received from their civil service contacts. They decided that 'the Department of Industry is deeply engaged in proposals for implementing Labour's pre-election ideas for reforming private industry'.[13]

Their suspicions were enhanced by a progress report of Benn's, given to the TUC-Labour Party liaison committee, in which he explained plans for planning agreements, initially with 100 firms, controlling about half of manufacturing output and agreed on a tripartite basis with the unions. They would cover price control, the level of domestic and foreign sales, domestic investment levels, industrial relations practices and product development. The report also included an undertaking to hold

> 'A series of meetings in major cities throughout the country at which we hope to meet local trade union officials, local authorities, shop stewards, and gatherings of workers whose support is essential if our policies are to succeed.'[14]

It committed the Department to a further Green Paper around which discussion was to take place.

The CBI was appalled. Aims of Industry launched a £100,000 anti-nationalisation campaign. The two proposals which most incensed them were information disclosure and the prospect of a broad extension of state ownership, particularly into profitable areas.

Wilson responded immediately. He was particularly annoyed at the idea that a government Department should campaign publicly, or discuss publicly, around its ideas before they were government policy. *The Times* reported that the document had brought 'bitter comments from senior [Labour] politicians who see it as electorally damaging', and added, 'strenuous efforts are now being made by the government to halt the damaging effects of these public ownership proposals'.

Wilson personally took over the chairmanship of the Cabinet subcommittee which dealt with industrial matters. Using this position he steadily ground down the Industry Bill proposals as they emerged. 'Private industry must have the necessary confidence to maintain and increase investment to do their duty by the people', he declared, 'and confidence demands that a clear frontier must be defined between what is public and what is private industry'. Wilson's own autobiographical account records that:

> '. . . it was essential that both sides of industry should know exactly where they stood, within what it was vital to emphasise was to continue to be a mixed economy . . . A special committee of senior ministers was set up under my chairmanship to mastermind its redrafting, which quickly decided that the document should be

> rewritten. The final draft owed a great deal to Michael Foot, writing within the parameters we laid down. The section on planning agreements was cut down to size . . . the role and powers of the NEB were strictly defined: above all it was to have no marauding role.'[15]

Planning agreements were now to be voluntary. The NEB's size was cut: its initial borrowing limit was £700,000 and it covered less than 6 per cent of government handouts to industry.

In spite of this the new draft provoked a barrage of protest. The CBI denounced it as 'damaging and dangerous'. It announced that it 'regarded as non-negotiable any attempt to subject the 100 leading companies to a planning agreement system'. It produced a document, 'Industry and Government', stating its case, and individual companies took up the attack. ICI spent £60,000 writing to its 600,000 shareholders, 132,000 employees and 43,000 pensioners explaining why the NEB should not buy ICI.

Concessions were wrung all the way up to the Committee stage. A member of the Standing Committee on the Industry Bill – after Benn had been sacked – summed up the process thus:

> 'I had not seen an operation quite like this before. Here was this Bill which was a watered down version of a White Paper which was a watered down version of a watered down manifesto commitment. And then three ministers on top of this kept bringing what were really wrecking amendments.'[16]

The end result of this process was the transformation of the Bill into its opposite. The NEB was virtually shorn of any compulsory powers, the information disclosure powers were removed, and industrial democracy ceased to be part of its terms of reference. It was put in the care of Leslie Murphy, a merchant banker, who defined its role bluntly and succinctly in his introduction to the NEB's 1977 Annual Report: 'The NEB's main function is the provision of finance for industrial investment.'[17]

The government concluded a grand total of one planning agreement, with Chrysler UK, to whom it gave £37 million to save its Linwood plant. Two years later Chrysler sold out its UK holdings to Peugeot-Citroen without even informing the government in advance, and in 1981 Peugeot closed Linwood.

The exorcists gather

With the Industry Act out of the way, the target was now Benn himself. Joe Haines reports:

> 'The whispers from the Treasury's contacts grew stronger. Only if Tony Benn was sacked, it was said, would the confidence of British industry be restored. If confidence was restored then (so it was argued) industrial investment would begin again.'[18]

The opportunity was not long coming. On 6 June 1975 the result of the EEC referendum was broadcast to twelve million British viewers. Three days later Benn was summoned by Wilson and dismissed from the Department of Industry.

The result was a culmination of a concerted media campaign to make clear that the future direction of the Labour government depended directly on the outcome of the referendum.

The real issue at stake was the authority and leadership of the Cabinet. Callaghan had negotiated new terms for membership of the EEC which the Cabinet majority argued should be accepted. Benn and the left dissented. There was a public rift, and the doctrine of Cabinet collective responsibility could not be imposed. Benn and the left were therefore campaigning openly, in the party and the country, against the line of the Cabinet majority. Even the PLP rejected the terms which Callaghan had negotiated, with 145 voting against in the Commons, and 33 abstaining.

If the referendum vote had gone against the Cabinet on a major plank of government policy, on what authority would the Cabinet govern? It would neither have the support of its own party nor of the electorate. The left would have been able to argue that their policies represented, not only the mandate they had received in the election, but the current majority feeling in the country. Their hand in the Cabinet would have been greatly strengthened and they would have had a case for making a bid for outright control.

In the event, Wilson and Callaghan were able to use the campaign to rout the left. They appealed to the Commons against Labour MPs, and to the country against the Labour Party. They made a direct bloc with the central section of the Tory Party. In the Commons they won, with Tory votes, by 398 to 172. The Tories' backers helped them repeat this result in the referendum. The 'Yes' campaign spent a total of £1,481,583. The 'No' campaign spent one-tenth of this figure.

The two-to-one vote in favour of the new terms was widely and correctly interpreted as a defeat for the Labour left, despite the presence in the 'No' campaign of ultra-right wing politicians such as Enoch Powell, and despite the Labour left's dubious decision (with which Benn did not agree) to campaign jointly with him. Wilson was able to use the referendum to strengthen his personal position in the Cabinet, and the Cabinet's position in the Commons. For Benn it was a major defeat. 'It was an absolutely major political reverse', he said of his transfer to the Department of Energy. 'The Department of Industry was glad to get rid of me; the Department of Energy didn't want to have me . . . it was a position of disgrace'.

Particularly galling was the fact that the referendum had been Benn's idea. He hoped it would re-enforce popular democracy. But it had the reverse effect. It was used, as De Gaulle and even Napoleon had used referenda, to shore up the executive arm of government at the expense of the legislature by being interpreted as an endorsement of the whole of the government's policy. 'We had two general elections in 1974 and then we had a third vote', he said later,

> 'where the Labour Party was beaten but the Labour Prime Minister upheld. And that third vote destroyed the manifesto and entrenched a Prime Minister in power who was hostile to it.'[19]

Benn's position was now very difficult. He was torn between the need to disassociate himself from a government with whose actions he profoundly disagreed, and his desire to fight in the highest possible places for those he represented. He discussed resigning with his constituency party, which advised against it.

This reflected a wider loss of political will by both the parliamentary labour left and the unions. Neither now offered any serious resistance to the Cabinet for fear of bringing down the government. The left-wing Cabinet ministers' activities were limited to fighting inside the Cabinet to uphold the manifesto, but they still felt that this rearguard defence was worthwhile.

The death of industrial democracy

Yet a strange thing now happened. As manifesto commitments were one by one strangled and buried many of them seemed to suffer a peculiar kind of fate, in which their names survived and they were eventually passed, but what came through the parliamentary mangle bore no relation to the original promise. The fate of the industrial democracy proposals typified this process, and at the same time throws much light on the source of the criticisms to which Benn's policies have been subjected and the problems he himself has suffered.

The original motion, passed by the 1973 Labour Party conference at the instigation of the Institute for Workers' Control (IWC) with Benn's backing, proposed that:

> 'Structures be imposed which will allow for the full exercise of the talents and democratic rights of the workers in those companies; that these include the direct election of trades unionists at all levels under arrangements agreed with and supervised by the trades unions concerned; the board of each nationalised industry must be composed of *at least 50 per cent* trades unionists elected in this way, and workers must have the right of veto over all executive appointments including that of the chairman. Workers' representatives must have equal rights and powers with other members of these boards and complete information concerning their industries and enterprises and be required to report back fully to their constituents and be subject to recall by these constituents.'[20] [my emphasis – A.F.]

In August 1975 Peter Shore announced a committee to enquire whether or not the proposals should be carried out. Chaired by Lord Bullock, it had three trades union leaders (Jack Jones, Clive Jenkins and David Lea) and three company chairmen (Norman Biggs of Williams and Glyns, Sir Jack Callard of ICI, and Barrie Heath of GKN Ltd), together with several lawyers and academics.

The committee reported back in January 1977 with the notorious '2x + y' formula, whereby boards would comprise fifty per cent trades unionists, fifty per cent management – and an independent arbitrator. Somehow 'at least' had been translated into 'at most' fifty per cent. This was not a small difference, as any shareholder and any trade unionist could understand. The issue at stake was sovereignty in the boardroom – *who rules*?

The AUEW fiercely opposed the new proposals. The TUC gave lukewarm support but called for parity on the board, which it termed 'joint control'. An irreverent management expert dubbed this 'bladder control', on the basis that whoever left the boardroom first would lose the vote.

Even such a mild proposal was greeted with shock, horror and denunciation. The American Chamber of Commerce (UK) declared that US companies looked at Bullock with disbelief and dismay. The CBI said they would not co-operate with the government's industrial strategy (!) if Bullock was the basis. They refused point blank to discuss three of Bullock's recommendations: the imposition by law of union nominees on the company boards; parity of representation between shareholder and union-elected directors; and the right of unions to choose their directors. A further compromise was agreed, but legislation was never brought forward.

There were experiments in a number of nationalised industries. The clear aim of management in every case, and in which it succeeded, was to ensure that worker-directors were chosen by the corporation; that they served in a personal capacity without accountability; and that the framework for taking part was acceptance of strategic company objectives.

But the *coup de grace* to Labour's industrial democracy proposals had already been delivered, at a special meeting of the TUC with Cabinet leaders at Chequers on 5 November 1975. Wilson again raised the threat of a reactionary Tory government if Labour fell, and the TUC agreed to an industrial strategy identical to the one with which Benn had been presented by his civil servants in October 1974.

The outcome of Benn's industrial democracy proposals was so contrary to the instincts of most militants that they rejected, not merely the Bullock proposals but the idea of workers' control. Arthur Scargill was particularly clear about this, delivering several speeches and even co-authoring a pamphlet to denounce workers' control.

Benn had already made it plain at the 1973 conference that such proposals did not extend industrial democracy and should be rejected:

> 'We reject as a party and a movement the idea that one worker on the board is industrial democracy. We reject co-ownership. We reject the phoney works councils not rooted in the strength of the union movement. All these are window dressing, designed to divert the demand for democratic control into a harmless challenge.'[21]

Yet this was exactly what his policies were turned into.

These policies were thus not those he had fought for. But why was it *possible* for the Labour government to reverse conference decisions in such a manner, without a clear understanding in the labour movement that a reversal was taking place, and without a struggle against it? Did not the original policies, even as conceived by Benn, contain the element of compromise which paved the way to their overturn? The original strategy rested on two important prerequisites: the co-operation of the capitalists and the unity of the labour movement. His policies were framed in the belief that both could be attained in the life of the next government. But this was not without effect for the policies themselves. Scargill's critique of the IWC approach was quite pointed and hard to answer:

> 'To the IWC, workers' control meant a struggle by workers and their organisations to encroach upon management power and to cut back the power of capital in industry and economy. It meant workers supervising managers. They agreed with G.D.H. Cole's view that the conflict over control which occurs in capitalist society underlies and is more fundamental than the wages question. Workers' control was and is to them an objective, achieved through a process, *within capitalism* . . . As a slogan, "Workers' Control" was itself part of the process of wresting control from capitalist management. *In practice the IWC argued for participation with real power and control.*'[22] [my emphasis]

With 'at least fifty per cent' trades unionists on the board as a negotiating stance, it was inevitable that the employers would treat fifty per cent as the *top* limit and begin negotiating down from this figure, until they had reached 'one worker on the board'.

The Benn/IWC strategy was not in reality a strategy for seizing control but a strategy for negotiating control: a trade union bargaining strategy. In this it was markedly different from the policy followed by other proponents of workers' control. The

Russian workers in 1917 had also put workers' control at the centre of their strategy, but saw it as synonymous with a fight for power. They began from the demand for a three-quarters majority on the board – a clear expression of sovereignty in the factory and enterprise.[23]

Portuguese workers, who in the 1974 revolution secured the nationalisation of seventy per cent of industry (although only to see it later returned to its former owners), had begun by occupying factories and had negotiated from a position of strength. Chilean workers' control had advanced in the same way.

These experiences all showed that workers' control was tied up with the nature of the state and its legal foundation, and could not really be won on a permanent basis without a different kind of state.

This showed up in the fight over the Industrial Strategy. First, occupying workers had met the laws of property. Before they could set up co-operatives they were forced to indemnify former owners whose property they were alleged to have 'stolen' – property built with their labour. They had to meet criteria of commercial viability instead of social need. And they were in constant danger of ejection by the police until they had met these demands.

Second, they found that government policy was actually administered by a hostile Civil Service. Real sovereignty in the factory, for the people who worked in it, demanded a change in the whole principle on which the state was built. The government would *have had to authorise workers to run industry, in accordance with social needs, as its legal agents*. The 'experts' should have been under the control of factory or delegate meetings, their appointments and actions should have been subject to veto or recall by them, and they should have reported to them, instead of as at present to their superiors. The government's policy was in fact based on the *reverse* principle. The civil servants were its legal agents to whom workers had to refer for permission to act. The civil service thus acquired a *state veto*. This policy was thus in reality just another form of state control, and not worker control. Scargill was not polemicising against real workers' control at all.

Indeed the strategy strengthened the hand of the state

against the government. Using its discretionary right to 'interpret' both the constitution and government decisions, it acted as an independent power. Marx had called the state a specialised guild with a monopoly of administration, which protected this monopoly by placing it at the disposal of the ruling class of the day. Out of this very profound critique both he and Lenin had developed their idea of a workers' state organised on the completely different principle of the right of all citizens to take part in the state and to exercise direct democratic control over it. But the Industrial Strategy did not enshrine either of these rights, and so foundered on the same stumbling block as state nationalisation.

Benn now began to meet the problem that others in the labour movement wanted to use his policies in a different way from him. This was possible because he had not framed those policies so that a clear distinction in principle could be made. This problem constantly recurred in his relations with the union leaders.

Benn did not accept that the union leaders might have interests different from their members. Yet, whereas he genuinely wanted to bargain for power, the union leaders merely wanted to bargain. After all, that was their job. And the defence of their jobs meant that they had to have employers to bargain *with*, and a government to bargain *through*. With the left isolated in the Commons, this problem came to a head in relation to that most Wilsonian of inventions, the Social Contract. Benn explains:

> 'In the 1974 manifesto – and I drafted the words myself – and even again in the October one, it said that the Social Contract was not solely or even primarily concerned with wages, but is a joint programme for social reform. From March 1974 right through for the eighteen months up to the referendum, the government was trying to deliver the repeal of the Industrial Relations Act and so on, and there was what's called free collective bargaining.
>
> It was when we came to the summer of 1975, after the referendum, that everything changed. Wilson had got his personal mandate from the electorate and the party had been defeated. Now, during the referendum itself, I remember a very senior civil servant saying to me – I asked about wages, and he made it absolutely clear – that there would be an economic crisis after the referendum.'[24]

The timing of the crisis was engineered, but it had real material origins. Britain faced the first world slump since the thirties in a terrible competitive position.

The pound was now 'floating' so formal devaluation was not an issue. But the crisis was provoked by massive speculation against an 'effective' devaluation – a fall in the official rates at which the bank of England and Treasury would intervene to save the pound. The interrelation between speculation and Treasury action is what gave the ruling class freedom to choose the timing of the crisis.

Hence, just as with the 1967 devaluation, the only effective guarantee against a collapse – using market mechanisms of control – was an onslaught on the working class. As soon as the 1975 crisis struck Wilson offered TUC leaders two choices: a voluntary incomes policy, or economic catastrophe followed by a statutory policy. The trade union leaders agreed to a voluntary 'norm' of a maximum wage increase of £6. After a passionate speech by Foot, the proposal was endorsed by September's Labour Party conference. 'The £6 limit . . . can only buy us time', said Benn when introducing the policy to the conference. 'We were not elected to nurse an unjust and inefficient system through yet another crisis . . . we are not just here to manage capitalism but to change society and define its finer values.'[25]

This encapsulated his view of the Social Contract. But now it was used in exactly the opposite way to that which he had intended. His own case against 'blind industrial militancy' was used to argue against wage struggles which, Labour leaders said, would simply lead to round upon round of inflation without solving the underlying problems of the economy.

Benn had to go along with the proposal to limit incomes. He had hoped that this would form the union side of a partnership in which the government would take its political lead from the unions. But the effect of winding down the wages struggle was to demobilise the working class altogether, and render it incapable of resistance in any sphere. Wilson and Callaghan now used the Social Contract just as its critics had feared. The union leaders were given the job of policing the rank and file to hold wages down, whilst reneging on every commitment to raise social benefits.

In Benn's view incomes policy was now serving 'to contain

the bargaining powers that the unions had'. But to his dismay the union leaders turned out only too willing to comply. 'The trade unions were deeply frightened by the result of the referendum', he said later.

> 'They felt that if there was a General Election the referendum result would repeat itself and Mr Heath would be back in power again. The Treasury thus felt strong enough to demand what it had always wanted, namely a very tough wages policy, and the trade unions felt so weak that they had no alternative but to accept.'[26]

The trade union rank and file now faced a united front of business, the Cabinet, and their own leaders. Every departure from Labour's manifesto commitments was explained by the economic crisis and the need to stay in office.

The final seal was set on this sorry alliance in 1976 with a parliamentary pact between the Labour Party and the Liberals, to be followed by a series of ever more desperate parliamentary deals as Labour's majority was whittled away in by-elections. From then on Labour's parliamentary deals served to constrain every possible initiative, and the government finally fell, ignominiously, when it became clear in 1979 that it would not be able to implement its promises of elected assemblies in Scotland and Wales – largely due to the opposition of its own back-benchers. Unable to summon up the courage to revolt on any other issue, they defied the Cabinet against – of all things – the right of the Scottish people to elect their own assembly.

The beginning of the end, for any hopes of expanding the economy, came with the sterling crisis of 1976. Benn had helped draw up, as chairman of Labour's Home Policy Committee, an anti-deflationary solution to the economic crisis. He argued for an expansion of public spending, for public ownership of the banks and insurance companies, of construction and of pharmaceuticals; and for a new Industry Bill with teeth. Within the Cabinet he argued for import controls coupled with public spending.

An expansionary programme was carried by conference, but in an atmosphere of unreality. Even as conference met the pound was falling through the floor. On 1 September it reached \$1.77, sinking to \$1.64 by the 29th, and \$1.55 on 25 October. Healey applied for further IMF support and raised the Minimum Lending

Rate to 15 per cent, but matters went from bad to worse. A senior Treasury official commented 'We faced the collapse of the currency, the collapse of the government and the collapse of the Labour Party'.[27]

The government sent Harold Lever on a special mission to Washington, where he impressed officials with the danger of a Benn takeover. An IMF team arrived incognito, fearing public wrath, to demand a drastic £4 billion cut in the Public Sector Borrowing Requirement.

With other left wingers in the Cabinet, Benn secured some concessions: the government's letter of intent to the IMF promised cuts of 'only' £2.5 billion. But it was effectively the end for any prospect of pursuing welfare state or full employment policies. The reversal was complete.

4. Rethinking Socialism

And MacDonald took the government. Now we ask; What next? How will the 'Labour' government proceed? If it does not have a majority in parliament, that does not mean its situation is totally hopeless. There is a way out; one need only have the will to find it.

Suppose MacDonald said this: 'To our shame, our country has to this day a kind of august dynasty that stands above our democracy and for which we have no need'. If he added that those sitting in the House of Lords and in other state institutions were all the titled heirs of bloodsuckers and robbers and that it was necessary to take a broom and sweep them out – if he said that, wouldn't the hearts of British workers quicken with joy?

What if he added, 'we are going to take their lands, mines, and railways, and nationalise their banks,' and there's surely more to be found in British banks than we found in ours! If he added 'with the resources released by the abolition of the monarchy and the House of Lords we are going to undertake the construction of housing for the workers', he would unleash tremendous enthusiasm . . .

If MacDonald walked into parliament, laid his programme on the table, rapped lightly with his knuckles and said, 'Accept it or I'll drive you all out' (saying it more politely than I've phrased it here) if he did this, Britain would be unrecognisable in two weeks. MacDonald would receive an overwhelming majority in any election . . .

But MacDonald will not do that.

Leon Trotsky
Speech to the Tbilisi Soviet
11 April 1924

As under the previous Labour government, political setbacks and reverses forced Benn to rethink. But this time he confronted more intractable problems.

Last time he had been in office in 1964-70, there was a simple explanation for the government's errors: it was committed to the wrong policies. Out of office, Benn had therefore launched himself into a successful struggle to change these policies.

This time Labour had been elected on many of the very policies for which he had fought. The problem was that it would not carry them out.

Last time Labour's failings could be traced to the demands of unaccountable forces outside the labour movement. This time it was impossible to ignore the obstruction of powerful forces within it. By 1976 Benn was facing a new set of strategic problems arising from this obstruction.

He saw the Cabinet's course as profoundly undemocratic. He had hoped that an elected Commons majority, answerable for its policies to a united labour movement, would defend public rights against private wealth and power. The opposite was taking place.

Whitehall was a loyal transmission belt for the demands of the wealthy. The Cabinet was virtually an arm of Whitehall, and had broken the unity of the labour movement by relying on Tory and Liberal votes to win its policies against the Parliamentary Labour Party (PLP). The Lib-Lab pact was being used to subordinate ministerial decisions to the veto of only thirteen MPs; and there was in any case no effective majority in the Commons for party policies, which were supported by only a minority even amongst backbench Labour MPs. The TUC leaders either accepted that Cabinet policy was the more practical or caved in to its demands rather than risk a government defeat.

The democracy of parliament, as Benn had conceived of it, had been reversed. The state served the ruling class, the Cabinet followed the state; the Commons legitimised the Cabinet's actions and the union leaders policed them.

The country was living under a disguised tyranny.

Benn felt this heralded the emergence of a new political philosophy – corporatism – with dangerous implications. Its belief that 'real conflicts of interest could be wished away by high public expenditure on jobs and welfare under managed capitalism,' called for

> 'a disciplined society where the men at the top in government, industry, banking and the unions would sit down together and

> work out a common approach which it would then become the duty of each leadership group to impose by law on its own constituency.'[1]

But the breakdown of the postwar consensus now made it impossible for such policies to command a popular majority. 'Those in all parties who believed [in] them became more and more authoritarian in their thinking and, almost unconsciously, began to construct the embryo of a corporate state,' he said in 1979. The main policy elements of this approach were:

> 'a permanent statutory incomes policy; legalistion to restrict and centralise the power of the trade unions; a semi-*dirigiste* industrial policy; a move to restructure capitalism within a federal Europe; the whole package – hopefully – to be entrenched by adopting proportional representation which would insulate a form of "national government" from effective challenge.'[2]

This made his personal situation acutely difficult. He was identified with the Cabinet's policies, and shared collective responsibility for them, yet he deeply disagreed with them. He was both a dissident in the Cabinet and a prisoner of it.

How to fight?

This period has given rise to bitter charges of opportunism and betrayal. He paid a double penalty for remaining in the Cabinet: the penalty of silence and the penalty of inaction.

The principle of Cabinet collective responsibility, which he fought vigorously but was eventually forced to accede to, was used as a muzzle on all ministers even when they were defending party policy. Benn's parliamentary private secretary, Joe Ashton, was shorn of ministerial responsibilities when he opposed the social service cuts in the House; Benn himself, and Eric Heffer, were threatened with the sack for speaking out on foreign policy – in Heffer's case against the sale of warships to Chile, and in Benn's case for opposing joint naval exercises with South Africa off the Simonstown naval base.

This gagging made it still easier for the Cabinet to claim it was carrying out party policy and indeed, many of Benn's own supporters thought his policies were still operative. As the *Workers' Enquiry* explains:

> 'After all the names were the same: 'NEB', 'Planning Agreements', 'Industry Bill'; Tony Benn was still in the government; the Tories and their press had still attacked the Bill vigorously throughout its passage through parliament. There were very few public signs of the changes that had gone on behind the scenes. It was only when workers were personally hit by government policy, by the NEB closure, by the refusal of the government to impose a planning agreement when giving out millions of pounds of industrial aid, that trades unionists caught a glimpse of what was going on.'[3]

Confusion reigned. Benn could give little help to workers who wanted to oppose Cabinet policies but could see no clear alternative around which to organise.

He considered resignation on several occasions and received conflicting advice. His own constituency party, which he consulted after being sacked from the DTI and again later, urged him not to resign: close associates such as Audrey Wise said that he should.

Several factors influenced his decision to stay on. He felt that his responsibility to those he represented was to fight for their interests in the highest possible places. He found, moreover, some freedom of action inside the Labour Party where despite Cabinet discipline he developed his alternative to government policy and much of it was put to the 1976 conference.

He was also able to put his case in the March 1976 elections for the party leadership. Wilson retired and the PLP held elections for a replacement. Callaghan, Wilson's heir-designate, faced Benn, Crosland, Foot and Healey. Benn's campaign, based on policies outlined in a mini-manifesto entitled *A New Course for Labour*, annoyed the party's left wing because he was felt to be splitting the left-wing vote. He got 37 votes, beating both Healey and Crosland, and gave his support to Foot in the second round.

But this did not detract from the fact that he, and indeed the whole PLP left wing, were unable to bring about a credible governmental alternative to Callaghan. No group like the Bevanites in the 1945 government challenged the Cabinet by refusing to vote with it, or put alternative policies to the House.

This took its toll outside parliament. There was no national focus of opposition for the trade union rank and file, on the lines of the Liaison Committee for the Defence of the Trade Unions between 1966 and 1970, which could link extra-parliamentary action to the prospect of a change in course by the government. Everyone who opposed government policy faced a bleak choice: back Labour or get the Tories.

Benn was unsure of popular demand for extra-parliamentary action against the government. Trade union militancy took a nose-dive. He felt this showed that Labour voters did not fully understand the 1973 manifesto policies, and that they themselves preferred not to risk losing a Labour government, whatever policies it was pursuing. 'Why doesn't the agitation continue when Labour is in power?' he was asked by Hilary Wainwright and Paul Foot at the Debate of the Decade four years later. 'Because', he replied,

> 'the rank and file of the Labour Party know that it is better to have a Labour government than a Tory government . . . Paul thinks it is the parliamentarians who go and persuade the rank and file to stop agitation. The reality is that the rank and file of the Labour Party do not want to put at risk the survival of a Labour government.'[4]

Yet is this judgement not somewhat naive? Most Cabinet leaders *did* campaign strenuously to dampen union struggles by arguing for voluntary incomes restraint, undercutting the main traditional area of trade union action. Although Benn refused to fight in the unions for wage restraint – much to Wilson's annoyance – Michael Foot at the Department of Employment was cast in the role of the Social Contract's chief spokesperson, a role that he accepted gratefully, using the full range of his oratorical talents to win union support for restraint.

Moreover the union leaders' claims to speak for their members, which Benn accepted as good coin, was never put to the test of a choice between real practical alternatives. If Benn and the other left ministers had resigned and campaigned outside parliament to change the government's course, a third alternative choice of government *would* have existed. In this situation the response of the rank and file might well have been very different: the fall-off in militancy was in part a product of the left's failure to oppose Callaghan in the Commons.

Why then did Benn not resign and fill the 'agitation gap'? Many argue that his conduct reveals a basic opportunist streak.

But this conveniently sidesteps the political factors involved. In trying to analyse the complex of reasons behind any event in history, personal factors should of course not be ignored. But every personal decision is constrained by a political vision and by the alternative possibilities opened up by it in the face of a given uncomfortable reality. Those who focus on the man and not the strategy invite a repetition of what they criticise.

The root of Benn's difficulty was that resignation opened up only two possibilities: ineffective opposition or an alternative government founded on a minority in the Commons and relying on extra-parliamentary force to maintain itself in office.

Two questions then immediately arose: on what authority could such a government rest? Would it strengthen parliamentary democracy, or could it weaken it?

In June 1969 a Labour Cabinet had been forced to change course by a combined movement inside and outside parliament. But the Cabinet had enough margin for manoeuvre to change course without losing its majority, and without provoking destructive extra-parliamentary action by the ruling class. The economic crisis had not been so deep, and Labour had taken office with a commanding majority.

Five years later, popular action by the miners had unseated an unpopular government. But an election had followed which endorsed the miners' action.

In both cases the *institution* of parliament had not been weakened because the Cabinet could continue to take its authority from the elections and the Commons.

But in 1977 this possibility was virtually ruled out. Labour's majority was almost non-existent. The state of the economy was much worse and the Cabinet knew that if it gave in to working class pressure it could expect widespread extra-parliamentary opposition from the banks, employers and the IMF.

The only way that this conflict could have been resolved in favour of a left wing Cabinet would have been by the methods which Benn had championed while Heath was in office – mass working class action against the employers and their state.

Indeed in its first six months of office, trade union pressure had already forced the 1974 Labour government to carry out much of its mandate without a Commons majority. Between the elections of February and October 1974 Wilson had made a coalition with no-one, and carried through a rents and prices freeze accompanied by a huge increase in public spending. He had jacked up food subsidies by £500 million, frozen council house sales, boosted dole and pension payments, doubled the Regional Employment Premium and presided over a 16 per cent rise in money wages, abolishing income controls and settling with the miners in full.

Yet if conventional parliamentary ideals had applied Labour should not have taken office. It had received fewer votes than the Tories – and, incidentally, a lower share of the vote than it was to get in 1979 when Thatcher took office. It had had no majority in the Commons and Heath had spent four days trying to persuade the Liberals to enter a Lib-Con coalition.

The measures taken by the Labour government in February 1974, in the teeth of the biggest world slump since the war, had run counter to what the ruling class wanted. But the other Commons parties had not dared obstruct them because Labour came to office in the wake of a tremendous wave of militant action accompanied by great public sympathy. This, and not Wilson's Commons showing, had allowed him to form a Cabinet.

But this was the very fact which had made the February 1974 government so potentially subversive of parliamentary institutions. In reality its authority had rested, not just on the parliamentary vote but on a vital expression of popular sovereignty outside parliament: the *force majeure* of the trade union movement and the moral authority it had acquired by ridding the British people of a terrible government.

In 1977 a resignation from the Cabinet and an appeal for extra-parliamentary action would have been interpreted as an appeal to intimidate parliament in order to recreate this situation. But the employers would not have bowed to trade union force so gracefully in a situation where, for them, there would be no end in sight to the attack on their profits.

There was a real danger of a confrontation in which capital took flight, workers occupied to protect jobs, the state was called in and the issue settled by force. Both classes would have sought parliament's support. Parliament would have been torn between support for the state and support for the workers, between the old legality and a new one: between order and justice. Only a minority of the Commons could be expected to side with the workers:

furthermore there was real doubt as to whether these workers would have constituted a majority of the population.

Benn could see no outcome which would strengthen democracy. Even had events not taken such a dramatic turn, there appeared to be no way a Commons majority could be created in support of a left government. Such a government would have had to rely on extra-parliamentary working class action to sustain it in *opposition* to the Commons majority.

Benn did not conceive that determined working class action in defence of jobs, backed by the authority of a left group in the Commons, could win over a majority in the country. He did not envision the possibility that a government of the left could, with popular support, create a *more* stable democracy by founding a new and democratic state and by placing both production and social administration under the control of working people.

As he saw it the threat of subversion would drive a right wing government to use naked and violent repression. But if the left formed a government, the right could seek to overthrow it in the name of parliamentary democracy. The result would be either a bloody defeat or an 'authoritarian government of the left', ruling by decree without the checks and balances of parliamentary democracy to restrain it.

In the last analysis, Benn could not refute the argument of the classical parties of order: that a government created by an act of popular will would remove all restraint on the exercise of power and lead to a dictatorship. Unwilling to risk the erosion of parliament, which he saw as the indispensable guarantor of democracy, he was paralysed while it set about negating democracy.

The root of his paralysis was therefore not personal opportunism but the lack of a means, within the framework of parliamentary democracy, to hold a government to the policies on which it was elected in the face of extra-parliamentary pressure from private wealth and power. It was not until the democracy struggle surfaced in the wake of Labour's defeat that he felt he had found the solution to this conundrum.

Origins of the alternative strategy

But this did not mean there was no evolution in Benn's ideas.

On the contrary, as in 1970, the ideas which he launched on the public when the government fell had already passed through a long period of gestation in office. 1976-79 were years of rethinking which bore fruit in public action from 1980 onwards.

Two developments marked these years. A broad left opposition to the Cabinet majority emerged around policies that were to become known as the Alternative Economic Strategy (AES). The basis of these policies was a defence of the positive aspects of the 1973 manifesto and the search for a non-deflationary response to the economic crisis – particularly the sterling crisis.

Benn's own ideas continued to differentiate him from the old Bevanite component of this left opposition, while maintaining an ambiguous relation to the union leaders. The convergence between all wings of the party around the 1973 manifesto had already given way to a division between a Cabinet majority around Wilson and a minority around Foot, Benn and the other left ministers. But the apparent unity between the Benn and Foot wings of the Cabinet minority was already showing signs of strain – as testified by the presence of two left candidates in the 1976 leadership election.

This left unity held shakily until the deputy leadership election of 1981. But Benn's later intransigence was in part a product of his reflections on the economic and political crisis of 1974-77.

Anyone and everyone who opposed Callaghan from the left had to find a response to the slump, and the sterling crisis, that did not involve deflation. The immediate measures that suggested themselves were: keep up public spending and social services, impose trade controls to prevent a balance of payments crisis, and control investment via planning agreements so that domestic production could meet demand and competitivity be restored.

But the question was: how deep did the crisis run? Would such measures get to the root of it, or did the crisis herald a new period in which the old strategies would no longer work?

The 1974-75 slump was a great shock to the Keynesian school which had been Labour orthodoxy since 1945. It believed that state intervention had done away with slumps and unemployment, refuting the marxists' allegedly outdated view that capitalism was inherently crisis-prone. If a large-scale capitalist crisis had re-emerged, it was likely that the demands of labour and capital would become less and less reconcilable, and attempts to mediate between them more and more doomed.

Unlike other AES supporters, Benn inclined to the view that the middle ground in politics was disappearing. As he saw it, each class was being compelled to try and shift the relation of forces dramatically in its favour. The only democratic outcome would be a victory for the working class.

This tended to rule out the old social democratic solutions and called for more radical policy goals. 'The one solution that no longer seems to be on offer is social democracy, the philosophy which has dominated the last thirty years or so,' he said in 1979, two years before the SDP was formed:

> 'At the end of the war, when we were enjoying a boom created partly by the war itself and partly by the collapse of our main competitors, the social democrats concluded that Keynesian economic management alone was sufficient to permit continual growth. They believed that growth would be easier if there was just a touch of central planning, and that with public ownership confined to the basic industries. This, the social democrats argued, would be enough to preserve full employment and permit a steadily rising volume of public expenditure. This would have the effect of resolving the conflict of interests between capital and labour, the recognition of which is an intrinsic part of basic socialist analysis.
>
> Today, after a succession of cuts in public spending plans as demanded by the international financial community, and with rising unemployment, there are few people within the Labour Party still prepared to argue that the social democratic analysis offers a way forward.'[5]

In his view the attempt to impose such a policy now could only lead to corporatism. His own attachment to public ownership strengthened and, unlike Foot, he was increasingly repelled by incomes restraint which he saw as a one-sided sacrifice by a working class which had not secured control over capitalist profit and investment.

Benn had identified a long-standing tradition in British labour movement thinking in which the most important feature was a commitment to democracy. He countered social democracy, and the growing monetarist trend, with what he called democratic socialism. He saw this as

> 'very much a home-grown product which has been slowly fashioned over the centuries. Its roots are deep in our history and have been nurtured by the Bible, the teachings of Christ, the Peasants' Revolt, the Levellers, Tom Paine, the Chartists, Robert Owen, the Webbs and Bernard Shaw who were Fabians, and occasionally by Marxists, Liberals and radicals who have all contributed to socialist analysis.'[6]

Yet, in trying to define a new socialist tradition, was he not writing his own dilemma into history? On the one hand he reasserted a lost democratic tradition in British politics. But he unconsciously left out of his account many great democrats who stood at the margin of the 'orthodox' Labour Party heritage because they had asserted popular sovereignty in the face of the violence of the English parliamentary state.

The suffragist and communist Sylvia Pankhurst, the Republican James Connolly, the Scot John Maclean, and the syndicalist Tom Mann were all representatives of great popular movements of liberation which had had to defy the authority of elected parliamentary governments in their fight for justice. Was it not this tradition that the Labour Party had tried to expunge in its proscription of the communists in the 1920s – the tradition of the revolutionary defence of democracy? Were they not the true inheritors of the legacy of Tom Paine, whose beloved American revolution had inscribed in its constitution the right to revolt against tyranny?

And had they not discovered, as had Benn, that any electoral system is only as democratic as the state on which it is based? Benn unconsciously omitted them from his socialist policy committee.

In his emphasis he gave expression to his hope that, despite the intensity of the coming class conflict, the British parliamentary system ruled out the need to resolve this conflict by resorting to force, other than that of controlled industrial bargaining mediated through the parliamentary ballot box. Did this not contradict his own conclusion that class conflicts were likely to become irreconcilable? If the postwar consensus had broken down, did not this open up the prospect of a no-holds barred struggle, at least from the ruling class side?

Benn's hopes of a parliamentary resolution were raised by a deeper analysis, which he now undertook, of the nature of

Britain's crisis, seeking to relate it to Britain's changing world role.

Roots of decline

In reassessing the relation between foreign and domestic policy he was returning to problems which had dogged British socialism since the foundation of the Labour Party and had lain at the root of Bevanism's rise and fall: the problem of its declining great power role; its relation to Europe and America; its role in the superpower conflict between America and Russia, and its relation to revolutionary movements in the rest of the world.

The question he had to face, along with all others on the left, was this: why was Britain's economy in decline? In particular, why was it in such a rapid decline, and why was it declining so dramatically in relation to its industrial competitors abroad, such as Germany and Japan?

The balance of payments problem had forced every Labour government to cut back on public spending and deflate. The failure of domestic investment lay at the heart of Britain's decline in world competition.

The two issues were clearly linked. Attempts to expand were defeated when imports rose faster than exports – because British industry could not compete. But investment collapsed when the economy was deflated. Labour's inflationary policies had attempted to right this by pumping money into the economy to create demand, whilst at the same time trying to take special government measures to ensure that investment took place.

The problem was that all such attempts had failed. Despite the fact that the Labour government was pumping around £3 billion per year into the economy in grants and subsidies, and even though it had accepted the CBI's terms for administering these grants (as Benn saw it, *because* it had accepted these terms) domestic investment in manufacturing industry had never risen above £4 billion per year at 1975 prices.[7]

Furthermore the capitalists persisted in their traditional response to domestic difficulty: they invested abroad. Between 1974 and 1979 UK industrial and commercial companies acquired £11 billion worth of financial assets overseas. By 1980 42 per cent of production by British-owned companies was carried out abroad, higher than any other country except Switzerland.[8] In 1981 long-term foreign assets held by British capitalists amounted to £84 billion.[9]

Benn saw this flight overseas as an abandonment of confidence in the British economy on the part of the business community. Further, it reinforced anti-democratic tendencies because it forced business interests to rely more and more on external agencies to discipline the 'troublesome British natives':

> 'There is a curious conception in the minds of some businessmen and financiers that if national democracy is allowed to flower, as it could in Britain, it would become so powerful a force for social change that it could not be contained by the British financial and industrial establishment, which would need to call in aid from the powers of capital in Europe in order to hold it in restraint.
>
> There is no need to feel pessimistic about this country. It is only the upper echelons who are licked . . . They are trying to transform the troublesome natives of Britain, whom they can't handle, into the subjects of a new imperialism. Imperialism of a more civilised, more urbane and bureaucratic kind, represented in their mind by the sort of federal Europe they would like to see created.'[10]

He soon became convinced that the possibility of British subjection to foreign influence had become an established fact. 'Is Britain a colony?', he asked in 1981.

> 'On the face of it this may seem an outlandish question. Thirty-five years ago, London was the centre of the largest empire the world has ever known. Those colonies have left us, but how can it be said that we have become a colony ourselves? And if so, to which empire do we belong and who governs us?'[11]

The 1975 and 1976 negotiations with the IMF, he felt, did not reflect 'economic realities', as Callaghan had argued, but the imposition of a policy decision on a subject government. 'Two Cabinets in which I have served', he explained in 1981,

> 'have gone to the IMF for bridging loans, once after the 1975 devaluation and the second time in 1976. The IMF sent a team to examine Britain's economic policy and laid down the most rigid prescription for corrective measures to be adopted before aid was made available.
>
> The IMF operates by seeking a "letter of intent" from a supplicant government before agreeing to a loan, thus forcing a

> British Chancellor of the Exchequer to pretend to be volunteering economic policy changes, having in fact secretly agreed in advance and knowing that only the pre-negotiated terms will release the necessary cash.'[12]

The increasing domination of Britain by multinational investment further weakened the political independence of its governments:

> 'These global corporations – in oil, engineering, and minerals – have long since outgrown national states in the sheer size of their wealth, income and the world-wide scale of their operations. This applies with equal force to those multinationals whose home base is Britain, since they feel no allegiance to the nation from within whose territory they grew. They perceive their prime responsibility as lying with their shareholders. They have the power to maximise their return on capital by deploying their resources without regard to frontiers.'

Thus although in theory Britain was an independent nation, in reality it was deprived of political sovereignty by the IMF, the multinationals, the Common Market, and Washington. Its constitutional structure, despite the semblance of democracy, left ultimate power in the hands of an entrenched elite basing itself on the 'feudal remnants' of the British constitution. 'The Central Office of Information', he wrote, 'described Britain until 1977 as a "monarchical state" and not as a parliamentary democracy.'

> 'If a government elected on a clear majority on a mandate of reform were to introduce legislation to complete the process of democratic advance to the point where it became comparable to decolonisation, we might discover that the Lords' veto, the prerogatives of the Crown to dismiss and dissolve, and the loyalties of the courts and the services to adjudicate on the legitimacy and to enforce those judgements, would all be available for the defence of the status quo against the parliamentary majority elected to transform it.'[13]

Thus for Benn the theme of democracy now became intertwined with that of national reconstruction and national political sovereignty. He was coming to the conclusion that the economy would have to be rebuilt in and through a struggle to overturn, not just domestic centres of power but foreign domination.

He was re-enforced in this approach by a growing disquiet concerning the domestic effects of British diplomacy. He had come to the view, in the wake of Heath's decision to sign the

Treaty of Rome, that many treaty commitments had antidemocratic implications because they were binding on elected governments. But it was particularly disturbing that the vast bulk of foreign commitments never went before parliament for ratification and indeed were frequently shrouded in secrecy because of the alleged danger to the state.

There was hence almost no democratic restraint on the actions of the state and its ministers outside Britain: yet what they did there had far-reaching effects on the British people. Nowhere was this more obvious than in the field of nuclear policy, both military and civilian.

Benn shared with Bevan a clear understanding of the relation between nuclear technology and international diplomacy. Through his work in the 1964-69 government as Minister of Technology – a remit which included responsibility for nuclear power – he soon realised that the possession of nuclear weaponry and membership of the nuclear 'club' served British diplomatic interests by acting as a bargaining counter in much wider negotiations, as he revealed when he dissected the Tory government's problems in negotiating its way into the EEC:

> 'He [the Prime Minister] went through the agony of negotitions before he failed in 1963. He did not fail because of the negotiations. He knows that he failed because of the Polaris deal at Nassau. At the very moment when de Gaulle wondered whether we had shifted from America to Europe, the then Prime Minister reaffirmed the special relationship, confirmed the exclusion of France from the nuclear partnership, and confirmed again the insult de Gaulle had suffered when he asked for a triumvirate to run NATO, which was denied by America and Britain.
>
> My interpretation is that at that moment, or soon after, the right hon. Gentleman, then a Minister in an outgoing government and now the Prime Minister, resolved that nuclear weapon technology was the golden key to lift the French veto on British entry. It is not part of the terms, but it is an essential part of the deal.'[14]

As Energy Minister in the 1974-79 government he remained in close contact with developments in nuclear power, and became seriously worried about the extent to which nuclear decision-making was shrouded in secrecy. In October 1976 a radioactive leak was discovered in British Nuclear Fuel's Windscale plant which was not reported to him for several weeks in spite of a standing ruling he had made in 1969 that all incidents in nuclear power stations should be reported to the minister concerned.

Through his association with the Technology Ministry in the first Wilson government and his term as Energy Minister in the Callaghan government, he had also been given a series of object lessons as to how private greed and public power could intersect to produce results, in the nuclear field, which were both morally reprehensible and disastrous to the public interest. In 1968 the Atomic Energy Authority had opened a search for new sources of uranium and, unknown to Benn, had signed contracts with Rio Tinto Zinc to supply uranium from its Rossing mine in Namibia. The contract implicated Britain directly in the exploitation of near-slave labour in a South African satellite, and flouted United Nations requests for sanctions following South Africa's refusal to grant Namibia effective self-determination.

Benn told the House of Commons he had been misled but, to his later regret, did not recommend the cancellation of the contract at that time.

His attempts to secure a manifesto commitment to cancel the contract failed in 1973. As Energy Minister in January 1976 he proposed cancellation to the Cabinet committee dealing with uranium supplies; the proposal was violently opposed and defeated.

Whitehall and the Cabinet right wing had ganged up both with South Africa and with a huge concentration of private economic power represented by RTZ, whose board of directors included Lords Carrington and Shackleton and, according to the *Daily Telegraph*, could furnish a coalition Cabinet from its own ranks. Moreover the decisions which committed Britain had been taken without the knowledge of the Ministers involved and without the knowledge of the public.

This secrecy, and the lack of public control, was even more disturbing in the military field. He pointed out that 'In Britain we have developed nuclear weapons secretly and without parliamentary knowledge or control', and began to wonder exactly what implications this had for British sovereignty. 'The essence of national sovereignty lies in the capacity for a nation and its parliament to decide to go to war or make peace', he explained in a 1981 *New Socialist* article.

> 'I believe that sovereign right has long been ceded in law, through a secret agreement with the United States, and in practice by the very fact that no limitation on the US nuclear weapons based in Britain would be enforceable. Yet every student learning about the British constitution is told how parliament won from a reluctant Crown the right of control over the 'purse and the sword', i.e. demanded and obtained the right to an annual vote of all monies required by the government, and additionally the annual right to renew or not to renew the military discipline laws which gave our forces their legitimacy. Now, both democratic safeguards have gone.'[15]

Until 1974 he had opposed unilateral nuclear disarmament. But he came out in support of it within the Cabinet early in the life of that government, and publicly committed himself to CND when it underwent a dramatic rebirth in response to Thatcher's sabre-rattling policy and America's rightward drift under Reagan. Because of the connection between nuclear policy and Britain's other diplomatic commitments, this meant rethinking the whole of the politics of the 'special relationship' with America. As the Bevanites had been in the early fifties, Benn was caught between the struggle of the two great superpowers and sought to define a 'middle way' in the context of a new cold war and a new world upsurge of revolutionary movements.

Like the Bevanites he was drawn to non-alignment, but did not distinguish between a neutral foreign policy and an independent one; between the attempt to stand aside from all conflicts between states, as did Sweden during the Spanish civil war and World War II, and the attempt to identify how the interests of working people could best be served in each given conflict. Nor did he take a stand against the use of capitalist armed forces in any circumstances, as did both pacifists and revolutionary socialists. This caused problems in taking sides in conflicts where either Britain's state security or Britain's diplomatic relations with other states could be affected: particularly in relation to revolutionary movements abroad.

He welcomed the birth of Solidarnosc in Poland, which seemed to point the way to a non-bureaucratic socialism. At Labour's 1980 conference he argued that the Polish workers constituted a better defence against the Kremlin than sophisticated nuclear weaponry. But along with many others on Labour's left he was concerned not to align himself with cold war anti-communist propaganda and found few practical ways to organise support for the Polish workers. He thus failed to prevent Labour's right wing from stealing much of Solidarnosc's glory.

He opposed a nuclear role for Britain but continued to advocate British membership of NATO.

He called in 1981 for the unification of Ireland and the withdrawal of British troops from Northern Ireland but argued for their replacement by UN troops – rather than accept that the Irish people should settle their own differences without any outside interference.

An important avenue for resolving some of these conflicts was suggested by the idea of a European alternative to the EEC. His approach illustrated the weaknesses and strengths of his ideas.

An invitation to speak in Lisbon under the auspices of the Gulbenkian world foundation and the BBC world service in 1980 let him paint a picture of a Europe united East and West and freed of Moscow's or Washington's tutelage. 'The dominant factor in European politics today remains fear of attack by both East and West from each other,' he said. 'Europe is therefore caught up in the middle of this impasse between the superpowers, both of which show signs of being paralysed by their own deep sense of insecurity . . . but my judgement is that both the Pentagon and the Kremlin are mistaken if they believe that the other is seriously planning for world domination.' Referring to the economic benefits of West Germany's rapprochement with East Germany, he argued that trade and mutual interest could draw together the nations of Eastern and Western Europe in a framework of 'dialogue instead of deterrence'.

He referred approvingly to the defence systems of the Swedes and Swiss who 'have a large citizen army that can be mobilised very quickly and would inflict casualties on any invader, without nuclear weapons or creating a military elite that could organise a domestic coup'.[16]

A picture emerged of a non-aligned Britain, seeking a non-aligned Europe within which the old superpower fears and conflicts could be set aside, breaking the paralysing and anti-democratic grip of the military and state bureaucracies of both East and West who relied on mutual antagonism as the excuse to hold their own populations in thrall.

The AES in a world context

This new outlook gave cohesion and coherence to his vision of the AES. If the British people were the subjects of foreign powers, the British capitalists' resistance to change would lie in cowardice or a mistaken understanding of their own best interests. 'The Vichy spirit in the top echelons of the establishment is quite astonishing,' he said in 1979. 'If you listen to those who inhabit the golden triangle of the City of London, Fleet Street and Whitehall,'

> 'there is a lot of defeatism. Compare that with the mood amongst shop stewards at Lucas Aerospace, at Meriden, at Kirkby, and the shop stewards' committees up and down the country. They may be angry, worried and disappointed but they are not defeated. Compare them with the gloomy men who go to City luncheons and dinners in their boiled shirts forever calling upon everyone to face the harsh realities of technical change. It is a sort of 1984 in reverse.'[17]

A 'liberation' struggle for Britain could aim to convince the electorate that British capital's own best interests lay with the Alternative Economic Strategy.

It seemed reasonable that a determined government could brush aside the resistance of a relatively small number of undemocratic institutions, and win over the business community by an appeal to national patriotism. The working class could proclaim itself the liberator of British capital from foreign domination, and once British capital realised the labour movement was determined to go ahead with its new policies, it would bear it and perhaps even grin. As Energy Minister, with a free hand to negotiate with big corporations, and when his department showed itself to be absolutely determined and implacable, the company negotiators gave way. 'I believe that if this [watering down] had not taken place we could have got agreement with all 100 major companies,' he told the *Workers' Enquiry*.

> 'I say this because we got it [agreements] with the oil companies – though we stayed up all night until they gave way. And we could have got it with the other main companies. Some leading industrialists had seen how they worked in other countries and told me they saw no problem in principle.'[18]

It did not occur to him that this apparent surrender might be no more than a tactical retreat. He left out of his account the fact that the oil companies have been accustomed to conceding control over production to the oil-producing countries.

The thesis that Britain was subject to foreign domination would also justify import controls, the subject of much hostility from the left, both because of their discriminating effects against foreign workers oppressed by British capital, and because they would force British workers in any case to pay a disguised subsidy to backward British industrialists.

The analysis fitted with the thinking of architects of the Alternative Economic Strategy such as Stuart Holland, and also that of the TUC. They argued that Britain had to adopt a 'German' or 'Japanese' model of socialist reconstruction, but in the socialist cause. In Germany and Japan the state and banks had intervened in the economy after the war, with the co-operation of both labour and industry, to build up the domestic economy behind protective tariff barriers. Labour could apply the same methods and gain an advantage over capital, it was argued, by controlling the process and dictating the terms.

Most important of all, however, his analysis suggested that a firm socialist policy would not stand in the way of winning a parliamentary majority and forming a parliamentary government. Socialists could expect an easy majority, unlikely to be disrupted by desertions and inner-parliamentary manoeuvres of the kind which produced the Lib-Lab pact. If the main source of opposition to radical reform lay *outside* Britain, the main threat to an elected government was likely to be that faced by Allende in Chile – *extra*-parliamentary attacks by a ruling class which really could not tolerate parliament at all. Socialism could defend its democratic legitimacy by defending parliament against the state, and need pay far less attention to the danger that the state would be used, not to overturn parliament but, as in 1974, to bend parliament to its will and provide a cloak for antidemocratic manoeuvres.

Finally, the possibility that a section of the leadership of the Labour movement itself might have an interest in allying with antidemocratic forces inside Britain, for short-term advantage and personal gain, was excluded by Benn's analysis. Instead, it suggested that divisions and disunity inside the labour movement could not readily be provoked by the ruling class, since only marginal sections of British society would have an interest in maintaining the status quo or frustrating change.

But Benn's clear and coherent analysis highlighted the pitfalls of his strategy. Supposing his argument was based on a false premise and the main source of opposition to change lay *inside* Britain? Suppose the bulk of the British capitalist class had no interest in taking part in national reconstruction unless the working class were first completely shattered, as had been the German and Japanese working classes before and during the war?

If this were the case, apparently 'foreign' intervention would be no more than an excuse cooked up, or even engineered by British capital to impose policies it favoured. In this case they would defend themselves *against* an attempt at national reconstruction, so that the AES would sharpen class conflict rather than overcoming it. If a strong section of British capital was strongly attached to the 'special relationship' with America, attempts at disarmament would be violently resisted. If British capital had established a foothold and an interest in Europe, withdrawal would put them in deadly peril.

If this were the case, even the quite mild reforms proposed in the AES would throw the country into a crisis, and they would be resisted to the last ditch. Furthermore, if these British capitalists were still implicated in the oppression and exploitation of others abroad, then a large part of the British people might well see themselves as drawing benefits from imperialism so that the basis would exist for a reactionary, racist and jingoist popular counter-response to radical change. Indeed this would be particularly dangerous if part of the labour leadership, with a following in the working class, was itself implicated in imperialism's activities.

If substantial sections of the population could be convinced that their short-term interests would be threatened by radical change, then the ruling classes would be foolish indeed to seek the overthrow of parliament; they would be far better advised to try to rig it, as had their European counterparts for decades, by means of coalition governments and by sowing division in the labour movement. Given their control of the state machine, and given their influence on important sections of the trade union leadership, this would be their most likely option.

In this case a strategy which insisted on capturing a parliamentary majority before offering a serious challenge to the state would place the labour movement at a permanent disadvantage. The capitalists would be able to attack working people with all the means at their disposal, including their state machine and their wealth, and the working class would have its arms tied behind its back by an endless wait for a majority in an increasingly rigged parliament before it could even reply to the attack, let alone promote its own policies. And in the event of a parliamentary victory the capitalists need only muster a few desertions to scupper the prospects of a democratically elected government, without ever having to resort to illegal force.

The evidence hardly supports Benn's 'colonial' thesis. Successive governments have had to bow to foreign powers. But was this at the instigation of forces *inside* or outside Britain? Most of the multinationals which dictate to British governments, even if through foreign mouthpieces, are British-owned.

Benn himself holds that the 1976 sterling crisis was engineered by the Treasury. Michael Meacher was to put it even more strongly: 'Professor Fred Hirsch asserted in 1977 that the IMF was largely the vehicle by which domestic groups, including the City, Bank and Treasury, could get extra power behind their elbows to jog elected Ministers'.

The EEC referendum result cannot just be put down to ignorance. The very scale of support for the 'yes' campaign shows that powerful interests inside Britain support the Brussels connection.

Furthermore, the very basis of the 'special relationship' was *Britain's* own insistence, after the war, on a continued Great Power role. It was Churchill who proposed a three-way division of the world between Britain, America and Russia at the wartime conferences of Yalta and Teheran. It was Churchill who excluded the French from nuclear technology. It was Duncan Sandys who later conceived the independent nuclear deterrent so that Britain could maintain a world role after Suez.

And this arrangement got more than marginal support. Indeed, Labour was implicated from the start. Its involvement dates back to the same wartime coalition government that produced the postwar welfare state consensus, which *also* forged a foreign policy consensus – a fact often conveniently forgotten.

'Bipartisanship' abroad – the ugly face of 1945 – survived long after domestic agreement began to crumble. It gagged Benn and Heffer for trying to stop warships being sent to South Africa and sold to Chile. It led Wilson to advise Lyndon Johnson on how to conduct the Vietnam war, on the strength of British anti-insurgent experience in Malaysia. It led successive Labour governments to prosecute a futile and oppressive war in Ireland.

Moreover this was buttressed by deep TUC involvement. The TUC international committee enjoys such strong foreign office connections that it exchanges staff and undertakes foreign office missions. Its doings are so secret that not even the Labour Party's own International Committee has access to them. A series of American/Foreign Office sponsored bodies such as the North Atlantic Committee involve or involved leading labour movement figures such as Chapple, Duffy, and many more.

The empire never ended

Such strong attachment to such morally repugnant policies suggests a material connection.

It also suggests an alternative explanation of Britain's decline: an explanation that sheds some light on Labour's crisis, the fall of Bevanism and the rise of Bennism. This explanation suggests that the last-ditch maintenance of imperial privilege, and not its abandonment, is at the root of the present crisis.

The economic background to the postwar foreign consensus dates back to the opening of this century, into which Britain arrived as the world's leading power, a position it then spent fifty years losing to America. In its imperial heyday it was the world's leading industrial power, the world's leading trading power, the world's leading financial power and the world's leading military power. These four roles acted in harmony. But by the turn of the century it was losing industrial pre-eminence because its control of world trade and finance encouraged it to invest overseas rather than at home, whereas its competitors were obliged to direct their attention to their own industrialists.

But this threw its industrial role into conflict with its other roles in such a way that a vicious circle was created. On the one hand Britain had tremendous control over foreign markets and investment opportunities, which yielded higher rates of return than domestic investment and there was therefore no incentive to domestic investment. On the other hand reliance on foreign investment strengthened all those institutions that disfavoured domestic investment: a high pound, making it cheaper to produce abroad and import back to Britain, at the expense of export industries; a reserve role for sterling and a strong overseas banking sector, discouraging domestic financing; a working class with high living standards based on cheap foreign imports, and strong union organisation resistant to technical change; and a military-colonial state geared to foreign investment or domination, and populated by the enemies of liberal industrial capital.

A reversal of Britain's dependence on foreign investment called for a simultaneous attack on all these institutions. By 1905, when a massive Liberal majority was returned on a popular working class vote, the road to a parliamentary solution was almost entirely blocked. Lloyd George took on the Lords, the unions and the Unionists at one go, and fell to a counterattack from two irreconcilable forces: reactionary Toryism and syndicalism. But every antithesis has a synthesis, and the Liberals were replaced by a Labour leadership forged in the 1915 coalition and schooled in the belief that socialism could be equated with wartime controls combined with welfare benefits paid for with the proceeds of Britain's world leadership.

This merely made the union and the Labour Party leaderships part of the same suicidal complex as the rest of British society. They could not attack the overseas interests which provided the cheap imports and state finance that paid for Labour's programme. They could not re-focus on domestic investment within a mixed economy without attacking their working class base.

The result was that after the second world war Britain embarked on a new phase of investment in its old colonies, while other countries opened up a world boom based on *metropolitan* expansion and *domestic* investment, under US leadership. Britain established a neo-colonial relationship with the old terrotories via sterling's world role, the sterling area, the Commonwealth, and thc postwar diplomatic division of the world into 'spheres of influence'.

Thus Britain's postwar prosperity rested, not on metropolitan investment like other Western nations, but on the maintenance of an old imperial role in a new guise. Britain did not retreat from its empire. It retreated into it. By 1967 British overseas investments had expanded from 1.5 billion to £12 billion – described by one economic observer as 'unprecedented in British history'.[19] And 60 per cent of this investment was in the old empire.

The foundations of the new operation were laid over 70 years before by the arch-reactionary Tory Joseph Chamberlain, who led the Liberal unionist split of 1886, and subsequently helped reconstruct the Tories as a protectionist-unionist party. At the centre of his scheme was the idea that Britain should enter into protectionist arrangements with its former colonies and economic satellites to defend British traders against their advanced competitors, whilst providing cheap food and raw materials to maintain domestic peace.

These ideas bore fruit at the 'inter-imperialist relations committee' of the 1926 Tory government which summoned an 'inter-imperialist conference' – and set up the Commonwealth. With this step and with the wave of protectionism that swept the world after 1929, Britain effectively abandoned Free Trade in favour of a 'sphere of influence' held together by the monarchy, the strong pound and British military might. The arrangement was described as egalitarian but, as one observer coyly explained:

> 'since the new egalitarian theory had far outrun realities, Great Britain had to be accorded in fact that special position within the Commonwealth which her history, resources, population and geographical position conferred upon her. Despite mere 'equality of status' with the Dominions she had to bear the main burden of imperial defence and foreign policy, she had the lion's share of investment and trade. Equality of function or 'stature' could not accompany equality of status.'[20]

After the war it was the notion of a 'British sphere of influence' in the Commonwealth that gave rise to the 'special relationship' and Britain's Great Power role. Britain resumed imperial operations as a US junior partner.

This explains both the collapse of the postwar consensus and the extraordinary tensions produced by Labour programmes which would be quite unexceptional in many other European countries. With the end of the postwar boom, the rise of movements of colonial liberation, and the steady encroachments of foreign competitors in overseas markets, Britain's overseas resources were less and less adequate to sustain the welfare state and pay for social peace.

Britain had become a twelfth rate economic power whilst attempting to remain a second rate military and financial power – and the contradiction was tearing it apart.

Attempts to resolve this contradiction in favour of the ruling class foundered on the unions' resistance to attacks on their members' rights; but those who sought to defend working people could now *neither* divert foreign income to social reform, *nor* offer adequate incentives to stimulate domestic investment.

The road to reform within the framework of the mixed economy and the postwar consensus was blocked. Britain was polarised between two irreconcilable forces: its moneyed classes, hooked on an overseas role which represented their only chance of survival, and a working class which could not defend itself without driving its masters to bankruptcy. In between stood middle classes who had become dependent in one way or another on income from Britain's foreign role, facing social disaster if this role was ended without radical measures to re-organise the domestic economy.

These tensions lie behind the downfall of Bevanism and the rise of Bennism. Bevanism was the left wing of the 1945 consensus. It could not sustain a challenge to Britain's international role because it could not face up to the radical measures needed at home if this role was to be abandoned. Whenever it did so, it provoked a ruling class counteroffensive which threatened to cut Labour off from influence within the parliamentary state. It chose instead short-term solutions which shirked a confrontation.

Bevan deserted unilateralism with the painful discovery that it would 'send a British foreign secretary naked into the conference chamber' – end Britain's Great Power role – and thus cut off the source of funds for the welfare state, split the Labour Party, and – as he saw it – deprive it of parliamentary influence. In the seventies his successors, arriving in office on the back of this betrayal, discovered that the price they had paid was subservience to the custodians of Britain's world role: the Treasury, the Foreign Office, the Bank of England and the Pentagon.

The *effective* project of Bevanism and its successors was that of buying social peace by paying for reform with the proceeds of Empire. But this practice was doomed from the moment when Empire could no longer foot the bill.

Benn's philosophy, on the other hand, arose from an understanding of the primacy of domestic reconstruction, and hence of constitutional reform – a lesson which he learned from his earliest days in MinTech. His evolution marks a process of discovering how difficult it is to do this whilst relying on the private investment mechanism, and learning the importance of constitutional reform to overcome these difficulties.

This made it almost inevitable that Bevanism should lose its popular base to Bennism, and that the result should be a convulsion in British politics.

For working people and their families, losing all the benefits Labour had brought them, and facing ever more repressive reactions to their attempts to defend themselves, the only political philosophy that made sense was one that concentrated on power – on fighting its abuse, and on winning it.

Bennism united all those who, like the early Chartists, had become convinced that the source of their misery was the abuse of power by the wealthy.

Bevanism, in contrast, had convinced its followers that their salvation lay in ending the abuse of wealth by the powerful. But without challenging their power, it could not touch their wealth, and slowly but steadily lost its relevance to a rising generation of working people.

In consequence Bennism came to represent the attempt by working people to press ahead with their claims at times when it became extremely dangerous for the ruling classes to grant them. Bennism has therefore proved far more dangerous for the stability of British politics than Bevanism ever was.

Yet this analysis also suggests some of the reasons for Benn's failure to deal with the manoeuvres directed against him in the 1974-79 government, and in the years that were to follow. For if, as we have suggested, the fabric of British politics is stretched so tightly by the weight of our imperial past, then it follows that the attempt at radical reform – even of an extremely mild character – would be extremely difficult to contain within a parliamentary framework. The labour movement's insistence on trying to resolve its problems without leaving this framework, come what may, could prove its greatest handicap.

For the ruling classes have extra-parliamentary resources at their command which do not require them to overturn parliament: their state and their wealth. Moreover, they hold in reserve the weapon of mobilising, behind the defence of Britain's overseas and financial role, all those who are dependent on it. Finally, they possess a secret weapon: the fact that the trade union bureaucracy is itself heavily implicated in defending Britain's state, both at home and abroad. This leaves open to the ruling classes the ability to use *inner*-parliamentary manoeuvres instead of *anti*-parliamentary ones; to use the *parliamentary system itself* as the device for dividing the labour movement at the hands of its own leaders – as Benn was to discover when, with Labour's 1979 defeat, he launched once more into the struggle for reform of the Labour Party.

5. From Benn to Bennism

> One portion of being is the prolific; the other, the Devourer: to the Devourer it seems as if the producer was in his chains, but it is not so, he only takes portions of existence and fancies that the whole.
>
> But the prolific would cease to be prolific unless the devourer as a sea received the excess of his delights.
>
> Some will say 'is not God alone prolific?'. I answer 'God only acts or is, in existing beings or men,'
>
> These two classes of men are always on earth, and they should be enemies: whoever tries to reconcile them seeks to destroy existence.
>
> Religion is an endeavour to reconcile the two.
>
> William Blake, *The Marriage of Heaven and Hell*

The Thatcher government was a much more traumatic experience than Heath's. The Labour movement was shell-shocked by Labour's disastrous performance in government. All the old certainties were gone.

Two opposed tendencies developed. In the engineering union the right-wing Boyd-Duffy team trounced the old Broad Left. It fed on despair, pessimism, and fear of the 'politics of confrontation', which many shopfloor militants turned from in the belief that the price of struggle was too high. In 1980 fewer hours were lost through strikes than in any year since 1946, and in 1981 even fewer again.

Union organisation was not uprooted: although unemployment ate into union strength, the proportion of those in work who belonged to unions actually increased. Bitter struggles erupted, beginning with the steel industry, and the miners won a real victory by forcing the government to abandon pit closure plans. A second trend became apparent: growing numbers of workers began to turn towards politics.

An attempt by Tory MP John Corrie to restrict abortion rights was defeated when a broad campaign, initiated by the women's movement, culminated in a mass demonstration called by the TUC outside parliament. CND was reborn and found thousands of trades unionists in its ranks. The Labour Party and the TUC adopted unilateral nuclear disarmament. National demonstrations against unemployment, called by the Labour Party, brought hundreds of thousands onto the streets in Glasgow, Liverpool, Cardiff and Birmingham and the People's March for Jobs from Liverpool to London won huge popular support.

This politicisation related directly to the Labour Party. In 1970 the demand for a radical policy shift came only from union leaders and constituency activists. The union rank and file were only tangentially involved in Labour's day-to-day disputes, because they were still ploughing the furrow of militant plant-by-plant trade unionism. There was no leadership struggle to animate them, and they were largely uninvolved in political activity.

This time, many Labour voters were unwilling to accept cosmetic policy changes. Now they wanted to know how to prevent a repeat of the last Labour government. Through their unions, they began to seek ways of doing so.

A convergent process was going on in the party itself. The very forces which made trades unionists turn their attention to the party began to drive its rank and file activists to look outwards, seeking not just new policies but new methods.

They faced a daunting attack on their traditional field of activity – municipal socialism. The local state could no longer sustain itself on local rates, and at the very moment when local services were virtually dependent on central support, the Tories began to withdraw it. A virulent attack on 'high-spending' councils was coupled to systematic attempts by Tory Environment Secretary Michael Heseltine to withdraw financial support and destroy the councils' traditional autonomy.

Constituency activists found their local role collapsing just when their doubts about Labour's national role were reaching a peak. A new brand of constituency activist began to emerge. Their philosophy was summed up by a widely-distributed critique of traditional party methods by Peter Hain entitled *Refreshing the Grass Roots*. Hain, a recent recruit from the Liberals, sought to bring his experience in the Anti-Apartheid movement and the Anti-Nazi League into the constituencies. He proposed that mass, extra-parliamentary campaigning should be widely adopted as a substitute for a moribund electoralism that had brought the retreat of 1974-79 and seemed unable to prevent Heseltine's onslaught.

Two pillars of Labour's broad church were crumbling: militant but apolitical trade unionism and passive electoralism. Would they bring it down? The first reaction was to try and reform it, and it was thus inevitable that three paths should again cross: those of the union rank and file, the constituency activists, and Tony Benn. In the process, a new movement was born.

Democracy: Third encounter

The Labour Party fared very differently from in 1970. It stopped shrinking and in 1980 registered 80,000 new members. This did not reflect trust or faith in the leadership, however. The constituency Labour Parties swung sharply to the left. New left wing groupings began to surface, such as the Labour Co-ordinating Committee, organised by a number of Benn's supporters around a new magazine, *Labour Activist*. In May 1980 the LCC sponsored a public debate in Central Hall, Westminster. Benn, Stuart Holland and Audrey Wise on the one hand opposed Paul Foot of the Socialist Workers Party, Tariq Ali of the International Marxist Group, and Hilary Wainwright, a co-author of *Beyond the Fragments*[1] – a popular book which drew on the experience of the feminist movement to criticise both the Labour Party and far left organisations. The debate, which hinged on the relation between parliamentary and popular action, drew an audience of over two thousand and gave rise to both a book and a record, indicating the breadth of current involvement in discussion on basic policy questions.

However, the issue which was to prove most explosive was that of internal party democracy. The Campaign for Labour Party Democracy, a small but broad-based body, was set up after Wilson vetoed the promise to nationalise 25 leading companies from the proposed 1973 manifesto. At Labour's 1973 conference over 200 attended the campaign's inaugural meeting. The issue uppermost in delegates' minds was clearly the accountability of their MPs. This became CLPD's first concern, and at the 1974 conference the call for mandatory reselection first appeared on the agenda. It fell against NEC opposition and at successive conferences resolutions on the issue were put forward by 12, 45, and 79 constituency parties. In 1977 Ian Mikardo pledged, for the NEC, to table a constitutional amendment the next year providing for 'automatic reselection in the way and in the sense' intended by the resolutions.

The NEC in fact introduced, in 1978, the so-called 'Mikardo compromise' which provided for reselection only if a party effectively passed a vote of no confidence. Resolutions insisting on automatic reselection were lost only because Hugh Scanlon abstained in a crucial vote against the wishes of his AUEW delegation.

The issue came to a head at the 1979 Brighton conference in the wake of Labour's defeat. The NEC reversed its opposition and reselection was carried by 4,521,000 votes to 2,356,000. This was the first time Benn supported the CLPD's resolutions.

It soon became clear that the issue was to become the centre of an all-out fight in the Labour Party, comparable to those of the late fifties and early sixties. The national agent's office 'discovered' certain drafting errors in the constitutional amendments passed by conference, thus providing an excuse to rediscuss the issue at the 1980 conference in Blackpool. Constitutional reform was referred to a Commission of Enquiry with six union representatives, six from the TUC, and Callaghan as party leader. Its remit included two additional proposals which had gone through at Brighton: to remove the party leader's veto from the manifesto by giving sole control over the manifesto to the NEC; and for the party as a whole to elect the leader, instead of the Parliamentary Labour Party on its own as had been the case till then.

Fears grew that the Commission of Enquiry would retreat from the decisions of the Brighton conference. If the proposals carried at Brighton were passed, the chances of electing a left-wing substitute for Callaghan would greatly increase.

The left now coalesced around the question of democracy. In May 1980 a united front, the Rank and File Mobilising Committee for Labour Party Democracy, was established on the initiative of the CLPD, the LCC and the revolutionary marxist newspaper *Socialist Organiser*. It resolved to campaign around three Brighton decisions which it now felt to be under threat: mandatory reselection, control of the manifesto, and extension of the franchise for the election of the leader. The battle that followed was to change the Labour Party, and the face of British politics, out of all recognition.

Benn's approach to foreign and economic policy did not, of itself, divide him from any major section of the labour movement. The idea of a non-deflationary answer to the crisis, the Alternative Economic Strategy, was widely adopted. Unilateral nuclear disarmament was adopted by the Labour Party in 1980 and the TUC in 1981 (though without withdrawal from NATO); withdrawal from the Common Market also became TUC and Labour Party policy.

To unify the movement around these policies the Transport and General Workers' Union got the NEC to call a special conference in May 1980. The conference, at Wembley, duly passed a statement – *Peace, Jobs and Freedom* – with which Benn, the TUC and the Labour leadership all agreed.

This included Callaghan. 'This is the basis of our unity', he proclaimed, brandishing the document – implying that the squabbling had to stop.

Yet even as his speech was relayed over television, more than half the delegates were flocking to hear Benn address the lunch-time founding meeting of the Rank and File Mobilising Committee. As far as the party membership was concerned, a new declaration of left wing policies was not good enough. They wanted to be sure that these policies would be carried out.

The hoped-for unity of the party dissolved as soon as it appeared, and there followed the bitterest internal struggle since the founding of the Bevanites. Benn was again propelled to the forefront of British politics – but this time as the leader of a conscious new left wing in the constituency parties and unions.

He had exploded his first bombshell as soon as the new government took office, by refusing a place in the Shadow Cabinet.

> 'If Labour is to recover its position it must withdraw from past involvement, rethink, regroup, and then advance again with a much more comprehensive strategy to secure its interests,'[2]

he explained. To take part in this process he wanted to be free and without false ties of Shadow Cabinet loyalty, expressing his own side of the argument as a back bencher.

He did not set out to provoke a split, or even form a grouping or faction within the party. He felt splits were ruled out by past history. 'The Labour Party always argues but it will never split', he explained in a talk to the PLP. He took his point of reference from the original purpose of the Labour Party, which was to represent all working people independently of other parties. Part and parcel of this ideal was that the Labour Party represented the *whole* Labour movement – and nothing but the Labour movement. Defections would end up in the camp of the Liberals, or their latter-day equivalents – but there could be no splits.

> 'The House of Commons Library prepared a list of all those who, having been elected as Labour members between 1914 and 1979, have defected from the party . . . It is a formidable list of MPs, including 24 ministers. But we have never split.'[3]

Debate within the party would eventually re-unite it around the conviction that it was committed, not just to worthwhile policies, but to carrying them out. In fact both the unity and success of the party now depended on this.

> 'We cannot convince others that we will establish social justice if we doubt our own capacity as a party, to adopt an effective policy or carry it out once we have adopted it . . . If we are going to be called upon to rescue Britain again, we can only do it through a manifesto approved by all sections of the movement and implemented in close co-operation with the party and the trade unions. If Labour is to remain united to take up its historic task again and to continue to advance democracy, [the] 1945 spirit of commitment will be required not only to convince the electorate that we mean to do it but, more important, to promise ourselves that we will.'[4]

Likewise he remained unattracted to the idea of setting up an organised group or faction. It was not until late 1980, and then under strong pressure from his advisors, that he even joined the *Tribune* Group. Explaining this to Robert MacKenzie he said,

> 'I refused [to join the Bevanites] for the same reason that I didn't join the *Tribune* Group until early this year, that I never wanted to be in a comprehensive group within the party. I always wanted to work within the party, and the Bevanites had a very tight discipline and whip of their own. Fenner Brockway asked me in the summer of 1951 to join, so that they certainly saw me as somebody they might have, but I took the view that the Labour Party was the right place in which to work. Looking back on it, I think that probably I got it wrong and that was why I joined only recently, after the Wembley Conference.'[5]

But Labour had united in the past around a programme of parliamentary legislation – not a programme of action. Now that change was becoming harder to win through parliament, could Labour continue to unite on the same basis?

Inevitably Benn's absence from the Shadow Cabinet, given the atmosphere in the party, emphasised the gap between the party and its parliamentary leadership and encouraged a more or less organised left to grow around him. Like an exiled pretender to the Throne, he became a focus for dissent.

The prospect of a Benn challenge for the party leadership became a backdrop to all the struggles that followed. Every triumph of the left was seen as a stage in his advance, and every step he took was seen as a left wing victory. The identification of man and movement was under way, and the first step had been taken towards the polarisation of the party, and through it the unions, into Bennite and anti-Bennite wings.

Why did Benn, with only a handful of other MPs, identify so squarely with the democracy issue, and why was there so much opposition?

Initially, he took a cautious attitude. With the NEC he backed the 'Mikardo compromise' at the 1978 conference. Labour Party democracy had figured in his strategy before, but as a secondary item. In 1973 he considered that the most important obstacles to progress by far were those outside the party:

> 'there are two blockages: one is the blockage in party democracy and the other is the far greater blockage in parliamentary democracy which I have described.'[6]

Indeed, he still saw these external obstacles as ultimately the most important. 'Firstly, we need to face the fact that what Labour inherits when it has a big parliamentary majority falls far short of real power', he explained to the PLP in June 1980, arguing that

> '. . . the House of Lords, the EEC, the IMF and American controlled nuclear bases in Britain represent four major obstacles to democracy and deny our people the power to decide our own future, or shape our own destiny. The Labour Party's first four objectives must be to abolish the House of Lords, to change section 2 of the European Communities Act to return the ultimate legislative power to the House of Commons, to adopt an Alternative Economic Strategy to free us from the IMF, and to control our own defence policy so that we can determine our own response to the international situation.'

'But', he now added: 'How do we do it? That is the key question.'

The key obstacle that had not so far been tackled was the autonomous power of the executive branch of government itself – the Cabinet, and above all, the Prime Minister.

> 'After eleven years' service as a member of four Labour governments, I have reached the conclusion that the range of powers at present exercised by a British prime minister, both in that capacity and as party leader, is now so great as to encroach on the legitimate rights of the electorate, undermine the essential role of parliament, and usurp some of the functions of collective Cabinet decision making . . . The prime minister and party leader must be made more accountable to those over whom he or she exercises power, so that we can develop a constitutional premiership.'[7]

But the premiership was the product, not just of the state but the labour movement. The key to 'unlocking the log jam', Benn now felt, was the mechanism by which the Prime Minister was selected and held to account by the party and labour movement. The democracy battle offered, at last, a solution to the problem that had paralysed him between 1976 and 1979; how to make the government accountable without having a revolution.

If the government could be made to follow the party's decisions by using the party's internal democracy, then the democracy of the electoral process would be restored. Electors would vote for policies, as decided by the party conference and outlined in the manifesto, and not for personalities. The PLP would be brought to account by means of reselection, which would make MPs far more sensitive to their constituency parties and less inclined to give in to the Cabinet. The Prime Minister would be directly accountable to the party through the leadership election. Finally, Benn argued, the Cabinet should be chosen by the PLP instead of the Prime Minister, in order to get rid of Prime Ministerial patronage. The combined effect of these measures would be a government that would actually carry out the policies decided by the party. Thus the *party* would become the means by which the government would be disciplined. The three demands of the CLPD were the best guarantee that this would happen.

A new test card

Yet this simple constitutional idea – perhaps almost as simple as the idea he had launched on the electors of Bristol in the 'peerage' election of 1963 – transformed the face of politics. Twenty years ago he described his battle to renounce the peerage as a test card, running through the British political system. Now the democracy battle played the same role inside the labour movement. It ran through the parliamentary party, through the unions, through the Cabinet, and from there back out into the corridors of Whitehall.

The establishment's reaction was, predictably, apoplectic. With redoubled vigour, the media bent to its ancient craft of branding Benn as the author of a dictatorial power grab.

The argument centred on an important constitutional principle which Benn challenged. In their eyes, and in the eyes of the labour right wing, parliament had authority because it was directly accountable to the electorate *as a whole*. MPs were representatives and not delegates. They were not bound by a mandate. Democracy was expressed in the right of every voter to remove, at the end of five years, a government she or he did not like.

Benn and the CLPD said that MPs should be accountable to their party. But this created a dual principle of accountability. Between elections the party would have control over the government which other voters could not share. Replying to this objection he explained that

> 'MPs express it like this: "once I have been elected to parliament, I represent everybody, not just the Labour Party." But in what sense does a Labour MP represent everybody in his or her constituency?

> Geographically, of course he or she does. Everyone in the MP's constituency will come to him or her for advice. Labour MPs must try to help all their constituents impartially. But we do not represent the *views* of the people who did not vote for us. This is a very important distinction that must not be blurred.
>
> In no sense can election to parliament give any Labour MP the right to abandon his or her political commitment or the manifesto policy on which she or he was elected.'[8]

A further problem arose from the fact that decisions in constituency parties, it was alleged, were taken only by a small minority of activists. 'The essence of democracy is the secret ballot and one man [sic], one vote', said Denis Healey in *New Socialist*:

> 'That was the claim of the chartists over a century ago. It is the claim of the Solidarity movement in Poland today. I believe it should be the claim of people who want democracy in the Labour Party as well.
>
> Too often, however, those who demand more democracy in the Labour Party want exactly the opposite – a system in which a small minority of self-appointed activists deny the vote to the average party member on the grounds that he is too idle or too susceptible to manipulation by the capitalist press to deserve it, and then deny their representatives the secrecy of the ballot so they can terrorise anyone they disagree with.'[9]

Healey's interpretation of Solidarity's purpose was highly dubious. In the first instance it was an oblique reference to the left's insistence on recorded votes for NECs, for MPs, and delegates to Labour Party conference. But the secret ballot is one thing when applied to individual electors who might be intimidated in a public vote, and another when applied to *delegates or representatives* who could avoid being made accountable if they kept their actions secret. Solidarity had never demanded that the actions of *representatives* of the Polish people should be kept secret – quite the contrary.

But secondly Healey either avoided, or deliberately misstated, an entirely different issue in politics; whether votes should be taken *individually* through postal ballots or polling stations, or *collectively* at meetings. The left argues that decisions taken at meetings with discussion are more democratic, because the voters can hear all the arguments. This issue is independent of whether the ballot *at* the meeting is secret or public.

Healey could point out that Solidarity drew more people into its discussions and decision-taking than the Labour Party. But its *principle of organisation* was the mass meeting and the conference, not the individual ballot and parliamentary chamber.

The CLPD could counter Healey's argument by pointing to the democratic links between the unions and the Labour Party, and to the fact that whatever their shortcomings, labour movement organisations tended to have democratic structures as workable as – and often more so than – the parliamentary process. They could argue that the way to overcome their shortcomings was to increase participation in them, which suggested they be given more power, not less. But this idea was another extension of the Benn heresy. It suggested that the labour movement might protect electors' rights better than the parliamentary process itself.

The real fear of the establishment was not subversion of the Commons, but of the state which drew its authority from the Commons.

One of the establishment's strongest lines of defence, however, was the argument that although the Commons did not at all times respond to the will of the people, it nevertheless defended their rights, and indeed that a parliamentary state constituted the best guarantee of individual liberty.

This is a vital point, which must be clarified by a proper distinction between democracy and democratic rights. Benn had shown that democracy – the rule of the people – was not enshrined in parliament. But he justly insisted on the importance of the democratic rights and freedoms which do exist – the freedom of assembly, of organisation, of speech and discussion, and the right to vote.

Support for parliament continues among wide layers of people who distrust it, because they believe that it defends their rights: particularly when they look at Eastern Europe. This support accepts the argument of the parties of order, that a revolutionary regime will make tyrannical inroads into democratic rights. Indeed Benn's own defence of parliament rested on the argument that it acted as a restraint against governmental excess.

But the CLPD argument was open to the interpretation that the *democracy of the labour movement and its organisations could serve as a better protection against government abuse than the ballot box*. The additional restraint of party control was needed, over and above the verdict of the ballot box.

This was not a revolutionary doctrine. It did not argue, as Marx and Lenin had, that the democracy of the Labour movement should be the foundation of the state. But the CLPD *did* say that the labour movement could control its MPs better than the ballot box had done.

This doctrine could not but provoke a clash with Labour MPs who regarded the democracy campaign with suspicion and Benn with mistrust. From their point of view it was a restraint of their liberty – and must therefore lead to a restraint of the liberty of the people, because MPs represented the people.

The Bevanites referred to their early days, when the party apparatus had been used against the left. 'At the height of the Bevanite disputes of the 1950s, for example', wrote Michael Foot in 1982,

> 'the fight of the Labour backbenchers – mostly left wingers – was to establish their right to exercise their judgement and conscience as socialist MPs against the detailed instructions of the party leadership.'

It was inconceivable, he wrote,

> 'that the parliamentary party should finally concede control over what it must do and pledge itself to do in parliament to a body outside.'[10]

Benn himself, in a lecture to the PLP, argued that democracy would liberate MPs from the grip of the Cabinet, and tried to win them to the cause of the party ranks. 'It is often argued that Labour MPs are threatened with domination by conference, or the NEC, or local parties,' he said,

> 'In fact the real problem is that Labour MPs have fallen under the control of the parliamentary leadership through patronage, official secrecy and demands for total loyalty to the leader personally . . . The media all tell us that what we are now debating is a widening gulf between the parliamentary party and the conference. But to argue along these lines is to misread history. The gulf that should concern us lies between the party as a whole, including the back-bench MPs on the one hand, and the parliamentary leadership on the other. No-one wants to see a Labour government weakened in

> any way by a revolt of the parliamentary party. That is the dilemma confronting Labour MPs. They are not consulted and yet they must remain a key element in socialist reform. That is why they must have a more positive role.'[11]

But would MPs see it that way? Their independence had been established in the earliest days of the Labour Party, when it was set up precisely as a parliamentary organisation. Keir Hardie himself had fought bitter battles with Ben Tillett, the dockers' leader, in the first few conferences of the Labour Party, over the principle that the parliamentary party should be free to determine its own course. Even the ruling class had intervened in the dispute, trying to remove union control from MPs by means of the Osborne judgement in 1909, which declared trade union financial support to be *ultra vires*.

The eventual compromise hammered out in 1911 gave tremendous freedom of action to MPs. They were accountable only to the PLP which had its own standing orders as an autonomous constitution. Outside periods of office it elected the Shadow Cabinet and the leader. It was in reality a party within a party, with very substantial privileges. Would MPs be willing to sacrifice these privileges?

The unions – or at least the union leaders – were also decidedly coy about Benn's proposals. They wanted to ensure that their own entrenched privileges, expressed in their financial control over the party, and in their use of the block vote to settle the outcome of party conferences, would not be eroded. They were far from happy about the prospect of a struggle for democracy which might spill over into their own unions – subjecting them to uncomfortable scrutiny from their own members.

Most significant of all, the problems of their 1975 relations with Benn now surfaced again. For them the primacy of securing a government through which they could bargain with the employers over-rode many other considerations. Now, however, they had an added difficulty – their members did not all see it the same way.

The union leaders were caught in the crossfire. For eight years they had claimed to support Benn's policies. Now they had the chance to fight for them. Why didn't they?

Their discomfort became clear at the Commission of Enquiry,

which included well-known left wing union leaders such as Clive Jenkins of ASTMS and Moss Evans of the TGWU. Jenkins even had instructions from his own conference to pursue the CLPD's demands. Yet all the union leaders on the Commission opposed NEC control over the manifesto, and only Evans backed mandatory reselection. No-one backed the idea that conference should elect the leader. Instead the Commission came up with a scheme put forward initially by the General and Municipal Workers' Union leader David Basnett, and proposed by no-one else – the idea of an electoral college. It was to represent the unions, the constituency parties and the parliamentary party, in specific proportions which in no way reflected their respective numbers of party members.

Constituency activists viewed the idea with great suspicion. Although it would break the PLP's monopoly of leadership selection, it was seen as an attempt to restore control to the PLP and minimise the influence of the constituency parties.

The Commission launched a complicated procedure for discussion. A series of formulas were proposed for allocating proportions of the vote in the electoral college to the various constituencies represented. This further endangered the chances of breaking the PLP's monopoly. Those votes favouring some extension of the franchise could be split between alternative schemes for setting up the college.

Benn was meeting the resistance of more than the parliamentary leadership. He was running up against the majority of Labour MPs and nearly all trade union leaders. He was challenging, not just habits of mind, but entrenched material interests. The democracy battle threatened to take from both MPs and union leaders powers that it was in their interest to defend.

Crossman, in his introduction to Bagehot's *English Constitution*, had explained the close connection between party organisation and the powers of the PLP and union leaders:

> 'Its [the Labour Party's] structure was determined by three conditions. First, it must have very large funds at its disposal; hence the reliance on trade union financing which led to a sponsoring of trade union candidates by particular unions. Second, since it could not afford, like its opponents, to maintain a large army of paid party workers, the Labour Party required militants – politically conscious socialists – to do the work of organising the constitu-

> encies. But since these militants tended to be 'extremists', a constitution was needed which maintained their enthusiasm by apparently creating a full party democracy while excluding them from effective power. Hence the concession in principle of sovereign powers to the delegates at the Annual Conference, and the removal in practice of most of this sovereignty through the trade union block vote on the one hand, and the complete independence of the Parliamentary Labour Party on the other.'[12]

Furthermore, this denial of real power to the party ranks was something in which the establishment had a distinct interest – an interest which they now expressed vigorously in their hysterical campaign against the democracy proposals in general, and against Benn in particular, who was singled out as instigator.

This was not an imaginary interest. As Crossman had pointed out, the party played an important role in the stability of the constitution, because it had to be relied on, with the decline in the powers of the monarchy, to guarantee acceptable Premiers. Despite the appeals of the media to the sovereignty of the Commons over the party, as Crossman pointed out, substantial powers had already passed from the Commons to the party.

> 'When Bagehot, for example, described the Commons as the place where 'ministries are made and unmade' and Party congress as the place where 'the debates are prologues without a play', the contrast was valid because the House of Commons in the 1860s still enjoyed effective sovereignty. But the contrast became less true as suffrage was extended and the modern party system developed. The right to appoint the prime minister – which Bagehot and Mill agreed to be the most important constitutional power belonging to the Commons – was gradually removed from it and shared between the parties and the monarch. And once it had lost its status as an 'electoral college', the House of Commons began to lose its collective will and finally became the forum of debate between well-disciplined political armies. Britain left the epoch of classical parliamentary government, and entered a new epoch of bureaucratic democracy . . . the efficient secret of the constitution was no longer the fusion of the executive and the legislature, in that supreme committee of the House of Commons called the Cabinet, but the secret links that connected the Cabinet with the party on one side and with the civil service on the other.'[13]

Indeed, as early as 1688 the 'Revolution Settlement' had ushered in the era of 'party government' in which the parties, rather than the monarch, acquired the effective right to determine the composition of the Cabinet. The question now at stake was: *in whose gift, within the party, was this right to be?*

The party had become, in a certain sense, an extension of state or Cabinet power. It had an almost constitutional function of linking the Cabinet to the ranks of the labour movement and bending them to its will. It would be a constitutional disaster for the establishment if this relation were reversed and the Cabinet were to follow the wishes of the ranks.

Matters were made even more problematic by the important role played in Britain by the two party system. Labour had spent more time in office since the first world war than the workers' parties of any other European country outside Scandinavia. On the continent, either the division of the workers' parties into two wings kept them out of office or, if they came to office, coalition could be used as a device for watering down policies and blunting influence.

The establishment's response was therefore twofold. First, it placed its whole emphasis on supporting the PLP against the rest of the party – in the process, making it clear to the union leaders that they would have far better prospects for reasonable treatment under the next Labour government if they likewise supported the PLP. Second, it began to investigate ways of weakening the two party system.

This was the background to the momentous 1980 Blackpool Labour Party conference. The keynote speech was given by Benn. It was almost wholly directed at the union leaders, and dealt with the manifesto issue – although its arguments were relevant to the entire democracy debate. He simply listed the proposals which the party had passed at its special conference in May – on the initiative of the unions – and showed how they had been eliminated from the programme of the last government. He argued that the structure of the Labour Party was such that the key decisions were taken in small, secret meetings without the knowledge of anyone except those at the top.

With this speech, he neatly turned on its head the argument which Callaghan had used at the Wembley conference to prevent the struggle in the party going any further. Callaghan had argued that the unions and the party now had agreement around a new policy. But what was the point, implied Benn, in a paper agreement if the unions left the parliamentary party free to flout the agreement as soon as it returned to office?

The trade union leadership was thrown into a visible turmoil by the speech. Television cameras relayed embarrassed union presidents turning, red-faced, to their delegations to disclaim any knowledge of the small, secret meetings to which Benn referred. He was bringing the reality of 'corporatism' to public view, and those implicated did not find it pleasant.

Amidst jubilation, the conference passed by a tiny margin its decision to change the party constitution to end the PLP's monopoly in choosing the leader. 'We have seen history made today', proclaimed Benn to a victory rally.

The victory was yet to be consolidated. In a timely demonstration of the importance of democracy in the unions, the CLPD's worst fears were realised. The AUEW, unable even with its huge block vote to prevent the decision to extend the franchise for the leadership election, nevertheless voted against *both* practical methods of setting up the electoral college. The confusion was sufficient for neither method to be adopted. Conference had decided that it did not want to stick by the old method of choosing a leader, but failed to decide on a new method. Fist fights nearly broke out in the AUEW delegation when angry delegates called for the casting of the block vote to be decided by a delegation meeting, which Duffy refused to call.

But a crack had been opened. The extension of the franchise could not now be reversed. The NEC convened a special conference in Wembley for January 1981 to decide on the form of the electoral college. It was a famous victory.

The empire strikes back

Benn now had grounds for hope. The left seemed on the verge of complete triumph. It looked as if only the last bastion – the PLP – needed to be conquered, and with the right wing packing its bags and reselection entrenched in the constitution, this would surely fall in time. This outward appearance of triumph led many on both sides into thinking the old power equations of the Labour

Party had been ended, and that it was now in the grip of small activist groups.[14] Accusations of 'infiltration' mounted.

But there is a difference between a fuse and a stick of dynamite. Small tactical matters had a big impact during those months because 1980 was a turning point in Labour Party history. Underlying social forces were balanced in an unstable equilibrium which could not hold.

These forces now began to come out in the open. The cracks in the Labour Party threatened to become gulfs which no-one could cross. Four decisive things happened after Blackpool. The SDP was born; the left's fragile unity burst apart; Bennism took on an organised form; and the right recaptured the NEC at the 1981 Brighton conference. All of these events were overshadowed by the momentous campaign which brought Benn within an ace of becoming deputy leader of the party. How did this all take place?

The banking, business and commercial classes were uniformly anti-Benn. Not one commercial daily or weekly newspaper offered him a platform. This did not even make good business sense, since his supporters numbered millions.

The wealthy were, of course, divided amongst themselves. But if anything this made them hate Benn the more. Thatcher had failed to deliver the goods. She had intimidated but not conquered the unions, while monetarism slaughtered domestic industry. Inner-city tension was building up to the point where, in the summer of 1981, it flared up in widespread urban riots. CND was mushrooming. Irish hunger striker Bobby Sands was elected to parliament and in Belfast council elections even Trotskyists were winning seats. Perhaps most important, though least publicised, Britain was still caught between America and Europe at a time when growing US-European differences made it vital to settle accounts. If Thatcher could not hold the right wing together, Labour could be returned in the wake of her failure.

But Labour had adopted unacceptable policies. It supported both unilateralism and withdrawal from the EEC. It was going to nationalise the banks. It seemed more against incomes policy than ever. And much more important, Labour's left had been formed on the principle that it wasn't going to retreat. It was assembling a trade union base that could not be trusted to remain passive.

Behind Benn even more left-wing forces were waiting, as Ken Livingstone's GLC victory showed.

A 'Wilson compromise' was not on. The left had to be defeated *before* the election. A Bennite-led party was not acceptable in government.

Yet a 'Wilson compromise' was equally unacceptable to the most militant rank-and-file trade unionists who formed Benn's union base. They had explored the farthest limits of their postwar tradition, which used local and sectoral militancy in the factory, and trusted politics to the Labour Party. The Wilson-Callaghan government showed the Labour Party could not be trusted with politics. Now, Thatcher was sounding the death-knell of local and sectoral militancy. Leyland workers were ground down and politically defeated – with the compliance of their own leaders – by threats of total closure to which they had no political reply.

From their point of view Benn's policies were the *only* acceptable alternative. This made them extremely sceptical about a Labour leadership in which the old team still had a major influence. It further caused them to subject their own leaders, for the first time, to real scrutiny regarding their conduct in the Labour Party itself.

It seemed impossible to unite the party on the left's terms if Labour was to be a party of government – and impossible to unite it on the right's terms if it was to remain a party of the working class.

Out of this dilemma support grew for a 'third force' – the Social Democratic Party. When Roy Jenkins flew in from Brussels to announce the need for a new party, he was an object of derision. But it was now clear that the decision had already been taken by leading front-benchers, in collusion with the Liberals, to prepare a split in the Labour Party. Benn believed the links involved dated back as far as the Lib-Lab pact.

The decision relied on the growing fragility of the traditionally unified Labour vote. Labour had cemented an alliance between industrial workers and professional or state white-collar workers by means of radical anti-Toryism and policies of state spending. But this alliance was cemented almost entirely in Parliament, and was preserved by an inter-party consensus in which social advance *could* continue by means of state spending sanctioned by parliament. On the one hand this ensured that the militant left wing of the party never pressed its claims too hard, and on the other that the right could not block off progress completely.

The SDP founders reasoned that if Labour's traditional claim to be *the* alternative to the Tories could be dented, then with it would go Labour's traditional unity.

Benn was convinced the SDP could split neither the Labour Party nor the labour movement. But he sensed a second possible function for it. If proportional representation could be used to change the foundations of the two-party system, then the SDP could be used permanently to deprive Labour of office. The way would then be open for a 'permanent corporate state' in which the centre parties could permute endlessly while the real decisions were taken elsewhere.

Even without PR the coalition threat was very real. If the SDP took enough votes to deny Labour a majority in the Commons, the argument would run that a coalition with the SDP would prevent a Tory-SDP coalition, and Labour policy could be ditched as unacceptable to the SDP.

In fact even with a Labour majority the way was still open to a repeat of MacDonald's betrayal of 1931, which the Labour Party had been powerless to prevent. Indeed coalition need not even take place for the SDP to be used against Labour policy. A small group of MPs need only *threaten* desertion to force a retreat on the grounds of party unity. The SDP was a pistol pointed at Labour's head.

Benn held that the labour movement's historic strengths would carry it through, provided it retained the democratic advances of the last two conferences. His response was therefore to try and unite the party around its policies, and these advances. But this meant that the PLP had to concede its independence and recognise the legitimate claims of the party. An attempt to continue with a 'two-headed monster' with one policy in conference and another in parliament spelt doom.

But the party's right wing and indeed a large majority of the PLP drew the opposite conclusion. They saw party policy as electoral suicide. They, too, wanted to unite the party – by uniting their *own* ranks and then uniting the party around them.

The deputy leadership campaign represented the conflicting demands placed on the Labour Party by the two classes it wanted to reconcile. Everyone had to make sharp, and no doubt agonising choices. But when the choosing stopped there was a new left-right divide. The left had backed conference against the PLP; the right had backed the PLP against conference.

The strange death of Labour England

The first casualty was the uneasy alliance between the Foot and Benn wings of the party. Callaghan resigned straight after his Blackpool defeat, provoking an election before the new machinery was in place. The PLP now had to choose whether to appoint Foot as acting leader, and wait for the new procedure; or hold its own elections in contempt of conference. It voted two to one for the second option, and Foot now came forward as a candidate.

Within its lights the PLP was only asserting its traditional freedom. Traditionally the party rallied round the PLP. But those days were gone. The LCC, CLPD and Benn considered the move wholly illegitimate, and said so.

Benn voted for Foot, but in an extraordinary act of spite the PLP excluded both him and Heffer from the Shadow Cabinet. He was co-opted when Bill Rodgers left the party, but a conflict was now almost certain.

In both 1975 and 1977 Benn's constituency party had advised him against leaving the Cabinet. In February 1981 when it asked him to contest the deputy leadership, it was only expressing an almost universal view on the left outside the PLP: there was a flagrant contradiction between the Shadow Cabinet and conference intentions. The leading front-bench spokespeople were almost without exception opponents of the policies they were supposed to fight for.

The decision to stand was taken early on among quite a wide circle of collaborators. Although the announcement was held until April so that the campaign could not be blamed for the desertion of the SDP defectors, the stage was set.

What would the Tribunites' reaction be? Any possibilities of a unified left stance were dashed by Foot's response. He immediately raised the stakes to a personal campaign against his leadership, and challenged Benn to stand against him.

But Foot was as much the prisoner of circumstance and outlook as Benn. Two concepts of unity were in conflict – unity around the party, and unity around the PLP. In other times the dispute could have been resolved amicably, but now the hopes and fears of two classes were bound up in the outcome.

The fragile compromise which had brought Benn back into the Shadow Cabinet soon shattered. Benn had only to speak from the Front Bench to bring out the conflict. A furious row erupted when, goaded by the Tories' selling off of North Sea assets, he promised that Labour would renationalise those assets without compensation. Benn maintained it was party policy; Foot said it wasn't. But what was really at stake was the Shadow Cabinet's right to *decide* what was party policy: the famous formula which had governed the PLP's relation to the party since 1911 and under which conference would decide policy and the PLP would decide what it meant.

This difference again went back to the foundations of Bevanism. Bevanism was used to a very particular kind of social democracy, on which the Labour Party was founded: the use of parliament, and parliament *alone*.

The British Labour Party was utterly dependent on winning an election majority. Unlike other social democratic parties, it had never had to confront the possibility that it might be prevented from carrying out its policies by extra-parliamentary means. It had no tradition of struggle for democratic reform, or against the state: in complete contrast, for example, with Austrian social democracy which built workers' houses in the shape of forts so they could be defended in battle; with French social democracy which was born in the flames of the Commune; or with German social democracy which had been an outlawed party for twelve years of its early career. In the last analysis Labour's socialism was closer to Bismarck's than Bebel's. It was a laboratory-pure parliamentary state socialism. When it faced a choice, it dropped constitutional change to win social reform.

But this meant that a Commons majority was the *only* road to change. Discussing proportional representation after the deputy leadership campaign, Foot wrote in the *Observer* that, were it introduced, 'One road only would be barred: the road to democratic socialism'.[15]

This was a confession of despair. Taken at face value it meant there was no road to democratic socialism in France, in Germany, in Ireland, in Italy, or any country with PR. Its real meaning was that if the Labour Party could not win an overall majority, *it had no role*. Everything had to be subordinated to this aim, and no other road existed.

Given this outlook, it was inevitable that the Bevanites, faced with the collapse of the postwar consensus, should systematically lower their sights in order to maintain their parliamentary unity. In 1982 Foot defended the Callaghan premiership by referring to five manifesto commitments which were honoured, despite a parliamentary majority of only three. Yet of these, three had been revoked by the Tories at the time of writing, one (jobs in the aircraft industry) depended on military spending, and the fifth, the abolition of tied cottages, although about three hundred years overdue, hardly compensated the loss of a million jobs.

The practical implication was that Foot had to defend the unity of the PLP against the party. But Benn had to defend the party against the PLP. Between the two camps, no compromise nor understanding was possible, and the deputy campaign opened in an atmosphere of bitterness and acrimony. It was at times hard to remember that Benn was opposing Healey and not Foot. In truth, a section of the left – the *Tribune* group – was being obliged by history to pick up its bags and camp with the right, and the leavetaking was painful.

Many untenable middle positions were tried. The *New Statesman* put it in a nutshell by saying Healey was unacceptable to the party and Benn to the PLP, and calling for an abstention. But an abstention on the left was in practice a vote for Healey, and a furious row broke out between constituencies who backed Benn and their left-wing MPs who abstained. The Transport and General Workers' Union put forward John Silkin as an 'alternative left' candidate, but this solved nothing because there was an exhaustive ballot.

But ultimately, everyone knew, the real battle was going to be in the unions, and here developments were also dramatic. The union leaderships had to walk a tightrope between Benn and no government, or a government and no Benn. At the Wembley conference a good litmus test of the union leaderships was the proportion of votes they wanted to give the PLP in the electoral college. Duffy wanted 75 per cent; Basnett and Jackson 50 per cent. Labour's NEC wanted 33 per cent. The eventual outcome gave it 30 per cent.

Benn ran into exactly the same hesitancy he had encountered before. Most union leaders simply didn't want him to stand. Clive Jenkins had a mug specially made for him with the words 'Elections can be a poisoned chalice – don't do it Tony'. NUPE's Alan Fisher came out for Benn, but his executive made no recommendation to the membership. The TGWU summed up the whole confusion by nominating Silkin and voting Benn.

Behind this was the same problem as before. What the unions wanted was a government through which to bargain with the employers. Basnett put their feelings after the campaign: 'If the Labour Party is not either the government or the only creditable alternative then this profoundly affects the attitude of the trade unions towards it . . .'[16]

In other words, the entire traditional relationship of the unions to the Labour Party actually depended on its status as *the* parliamentary alternative to the Tories.

But this put the stakes very high indeed: for if the unity of the Labour Party depended on the unity of the unions, it was equally true that the unity of the unions depended on the unity of the Labour Party. The way was open to a completely new alignment of left and right in the unions, based on the divisions in the Labour Party. At stake was the entire project of British trade unionism since 1900.

A new divide appeared in the union leaderships. The right wing, headed by Duffy, Boyd and Chapple, backed Healey and kept an ear open for the SDP. The most coherent left view was expressed by Scargill, now rising to the presidency of the miners. Scargill was a clear exponent of using union muscle for political ends, and was casting around for a rerun of the 1974 miners' strike. In between these extremes a centre group under Basnett's leadership oscillated nervously, but by the end of the campaign had recovered sufficient sense of purpose to engineer a victory in the NEC elections at the Brighton conference for a coalition of the hard right and the *Tribune* ex-left.

Birth of a Movement

But even as this wheeling and dealing was going on, a new development was preparing to upset everyone's calculations: organised Bennism.

The deputy leadership campaign committee decided from the outset to fight on 'policies, not personalities'. As it turned out Benn was absent for a large part of the campaign because of serious illness and could not, even had he wanted, have made it a mere instrument or platform for himself. But the fight was in any case collectively organised and drew together widely varying forces which became, through the campaign, a serious independent force in politics.

The nucleus of the campaign committee was made up of roughly the same forces that had been involved in the Rank and File Mobilising Committee: the CLPD, the LCC, a small but energetic group of MPs and a layer of individual but influential trades unionists, as well as the newspapers *Militant, Socialist Challenge, Socialist Organiser*, and *London Labour Briefing*. Some groupings such as Clause Four and Independent Labour Publications (formerly the ILP), which had been active in the R&FMC were less involved in the Benn campaign or declined to support it, caught in the dilemma of the growing gulf between the Bevanites and the Bennites. But the small layer of organisers rapidly found that Benn's real active support numbered not just hundreds but thousands and perhaps tens of thousands.

Labour movement demonstrations seemed like a sea of red and gold 'Benn for Deputy' badges and Healey was heckled and booed to the point where his accusations of 'orchestrated bully boy' tactics became a *cause celebre*. Indeed the movement's independence and vitality received a backhanded tribute from this quarter. Attacks now no longer centred on Benn himself, but on his supporters. Healey's case was not strengthened when he named Jon Lansman of the CLPD as ringleader at a demonstration Lansman did not even attend.

The campaign not only established Bennism's independence beyond doubt, but began to give it organised form. 'Tom Jackson wrote to Ron Hayward and protested that I'd gone to Brighton to speak', Benn explained,

> 'as if somehow there was a five mile limit which said, "while we're meeting, we're not having any politicians attending in this area, because it is an intrusion into the private affairs of the UCW [Union of Communications Workers]". Now the effect of that in stimulating the broad left in the UCW was formidable. And if you look around at the broad lefts, they're developing now very rapidly.'[17]

The campaign gave expression to social discontent whose breadth caught even the media off guard. When it began the pundits were speculating on a Silkin-Healey runoff. By the end the result had to rank as the closest in party history.

And so it was that, twenty-four years after Bevan's infamous Corn Exchange speech, delegates now gathered for the 1981 Brighton Conference. For the first time in history delegates assembled on a Sunday – to conduct the leadership election. The actors in the drama were all present. At the front of the hall, as appropriate, the union delegations. Around them, the constituencies. Almost huddled together in the centre, the MPs. Overlooking it all, the press. Outside, the paper sellers – and the public.

Excitement was at a fever pitch. The left wingers had been sorely disappointed by the loss of NUPE's vote on a branch ballot. They had counted on the support of a union whose leaders had been prominent in the campaign and which had led the opposition to Callaghan's pay policy in 1979. But they were jubilant at the sudden announcement, by the TGWU, that its vote in the second ballot would go to Benn. They were furious and confused at their MPs for abstaining: 'Why don't you stand, Neil,' said one delegate to the Tribunite MP Neil Kinnock, 'then everyone can abstain'. In truth, the race was so close that the result could not be predicted.

The days immediately preceding the ballot had been dominated by intense media speculation and bitter denunciations. The left and right alike were accused of anti-democratic practices during the diverse and often byzantine processes by which the unions had decided how to cast their votes.

In the first ballot, Healey secured 45.37 per cent, Benn 36.63 per cent, and Silkin 18 per cent. The real significance of Silkin's candidature would now be tested: if it was a left wing vote, Benn would win. If it divided or abstained, he would lose. He lost.

But so close was the final vote that the feeling of 'being robbed' was inevitable. With 49.574 per cent of the votes, defeated by the votes of MPs who left for the SDP within weeks, Benn's supporters felt quite justified in venting their wrath on their MPs.

But the underlying trend at conference was *already* to set it on a course that would have been at odds with a Benn victory. The election was Bennism's hour of greatest triumph – but it also signalled a turning of the tide. A pattern of advance for the right and restreat for the left now began to set in. A shrewd tactical move by Foot ensured that, although a vote to place the manifesto under NEC control was passed, it could not enter the constitution. Unilateralism was reaffirmed – but did not get the two-thirds majority needed to ensure it went in the manifesto. Most significant of all, the NEC elections for the first time in years resulted in a defeat for the left.

The union leaderships were at last coming off the fence. At Blackpool they had been uncertain, divided, caught off balance. Now the centre bloc had been consolidated and it knew what it wanted. It wanted a Foot-Healey alliance in parliament, in the party, and in the government – and it wanted a government acceptable to capital. Above all it wanted Benn to keep quiet, stop rocking the boat, and – not least – stop stirring up their members. But Labour's boat was being rocked by winds from distant places.

Epilogue

> To be or not to be – that is the question;
> whether 'tis nobler in the mind to suffer
> the slings and arrows of outrageous fortune,
> or take arms against a sea of troubles, and by opposing, end them?
> . . . conscience does make cowards of us all;
> and thus the native hue of resolution
> is sicklied o'er with the pale cast of thought
> and enterprises of great pitch and moment
> with this regard, their currents turn awry
> and lose the name of action.

William Shakespeare, *Hamlet*, Act 3, Scene I.

This book ends with the deputy leadership campaign. But that is anything but the end of the story. I have tried to give Tony Benn space for his own views in the interview which follows. It was conducted in late December 1981, after the enquiry into *Militant*, the blocking of Tariq Ali's membership and Peter Tatchell's candidacy in Bermondsey, and before the Bishop's Stortford conference and the 'declaration of truce' in the Labour Party.

One other task remains: to assess Bennism's contribution to the labour movement and politics in general.

We should begin by asking a simple question. Why has Benn been the object of such abuse? We have compared his treatment to that of a heretic: his ideas are not discussed, but dismissed. For him is reserved the venom normally dished out to Trotskyists, Republicans and Satanists. This is a sort of backhanded flattery: if an argument can't be discussed it probably can't be answered. But there are many unanswerable arguments knocking about Britain. What is so dangerous about Benn's?

Norman Tebbit has been good enough to offer a clue. In a

fury at Benn's endorsement of a 3000-strong lobby of parliament by Youth Opportunities Scheme employees, he denounced Benn for stirring up trouble amongst the jobless for his own ends. 'This sort of lobby is set up,' he said, 'by people who very skilfully make demands which they know no reasonable persons could agree to.' In other words, Benn is dangerous because he might be believed. Like the pied piper he casts his spell, and we lose our reason. We too become heretics: non-people.

The cowardice which refuses to discuss with Benn has been extended by Mr Tebbit; on this basis he need not debate anyone who listens to Mr Benn. More pertinently he need not debate anyone who opposes Mr Tebbit. There are likely to be many such people: the demands which no reasonable person could agree to were a trade union wage and the right to a job.

Mr Tebbit's line of argument leads to the gem delivered to the press by the commander of the Salvadorean forces in Chalatenango province, when asked why his troops were shooting citizens at random. Everyone here is in contact with the guerillas, he said, none of them are civilians. Mr Tebbit leads the way to a new concept in democracy: rule by the consent of everyone who consents. The fact is that Benn draws attention to an uncomfortable truth: we do not live in a democracy. We, the people, don't rule – and those who do want to protect their power by redefining the people.

Benn has not made a great discovery. In an opinion poll as to whether the British people govern Britain, the answer would be 'No'. Yet if the same poll asked 'do we live in a democracy?' the answer would be a resounding 'Yes'. How is this contradiction possible and how does it relate to Benn? Largely, I think, because the labour movement has won valuable freedoms: that is, democratic rights. When people say we live in a democracy they do not mean, in the old Greek sense, that the people rule; they mean that the people enjoy freedoms.

The debate which Benn has opened up is this: can our freedoms be defended without creating a true democracy? Can a people be free if it does not rule itself?

As I have tried to show, this is a very old debate, and those in power always seem to protect their rule by pretending to be guardians of freedom. Is not this debate opening now because this claim is being put to the test? We are losing our freedoms, even such as we had: the right to work; the right to organise in unions; the right of citizenship; rights of equality; the right to demonstrate. Our rulers no longer think them 'reasonable'. The Benn heresy cries out against this.

But the debate is conducted in the press and Commons with an urbane hypocrisy that sometimes takes the breath away. Two news items illustrate this point. In March 1982 a furore erupted over rabid extremist Pat Wall's threat to defend parliament against an attack by the state. Pat Wall, we heard, is a menace to parliamentary democracy and shouldn't be an MP. Different treatment was given a Mr Derek Cole, a Liberal and headmaster of an independent school in Sussex. In February 1982 he wrote to Labour's education spokesperson, Neil Kinnock, to say his school would oppose Labour education policy and that he had 'every confidence that we would, in due course, be joined in defying your authority by Conservative and Alliance education authorities and, I very much hope, by the armed forces in hurling you from office.' Needless to say Mr Cole's beliefs were not denounced as a threat to our way of life and Norman Tebbit accused him neither of raising false hopes amongst the youth, nor of demanding things no reasonable person could agree to.

Thus Mr Wall who wants to defend parliament against a coup is a danger to democracy; Mr Cole who writes to parliament threatening it with a coup is a defender of freedom. In what kind of logic do these propositions combine to make a truth? Only one in which, when one speaks of parliamentary democracy, *one really means the state*. Mr Wall is an extremist because he wants to attack the state; Mr Cole is a patriot because he wants to use it.

The issue of parliament, and the issue of democracy, are, for the establishment, secondary. The Benn heresy dissents. The heretics say democracy comes first. They deny the parliamentary state the unchallenged right to speak for them, and defend themselves against it when it encroaches on their freedom. They defend justice against order.

Small wonder that Benn can find historical precedents for his outlook. It has been the basis of every movement for radical democracy since Spartacus.

But does this make Benn a revolutionary? I want to defend

him against this charge for three reasons: first, because it is false; second, because I think when he fails his followers, it is *because* he is not a revolutionary; and third, because I think there is a distinct revolutionary socialist tradition in British politics. It is a consistently democratic tradition, and it deserves to be properly stated and properly understood.

Doubt has been cast on this last point by the record of Eastern European countries. But are these countries Marxist and socialist, or a perversion of Marxism and socialism?

Marxism and democracy

Marxism itself was born in the democratic struggle against absolutism and feudalism. It adopted socialism not as an alternative to democracy but as the only way to get it. As long as private wealth persisted, reasoned the socialists, so would private power. A classless society was the road to true democracy.

The Communist Manifesto's programme opens with the ringing words, 'the first task of the proletariat is to win the battle for democracy by raising itself to the level of ruling class.'

Marx and Engels greeted the Paris Commune of 1871 with enthusiastic support for its democratic methods, which they saw as the potential foundation of the new social order they had discussed in the manifesto. Here was a form of state, they said, in which the whole people were involved instead of a special minority. They pointed to elections of all state officials with right of recall, the limitation of officials' wages to the average wage, the right of all citizens to bear arms and to take part in the state, and so on. In spite of the limited inroads made by the Commune against property, they said that this was what they meant by the dictatorship of the proletariat.

The Russian bolsheviks sought to build a state on the model of the Commune, making soviets (factory and neighbourhood councils) the basis of the constitution. Their early achievements were destroyed in the catastrophe of Stalinism, but these achievements cannot be denied.

Benn complains that British state decisions to go to war are not put to parliament. The bolsheviks, however, put their decision on war or peace with the Germans to a vote of all the soviets in

Russia, one by one, and this while the war was in progress. Benn complains about state secrets. The bolsheviks published every foreign treaty in the government archives, to the embarrassment of all Western governments. Nor has Stalinism completely destroyed this potential: Solidarnosc has given us a glimpse of the *real* possibilities for workers' control in a country where private capital has been destroyed.

Marx's and Lenin's thesis was that the *first* step to socialism was the creation of a democratic state. The root of Marx's political philosophy is to be found in his *Critique of Hegel's Philosophy of Right*[1] where he argues that the state, as a closed corporate guild with a monopoly of administration, substitutes its private interest for the public interest by claiming to speak for a general interest that does not exist. This general interest does not exist because of class division.

First, therefore, the state in practice serves one class against the others; second, democracy is only possible if the state's monopoly of administration is abolished and it is replaced by a state involving all working people and their families on an equal basis; third, a stable democracy can only arise if the new state reorganises production and social administration under worker control so as to eliminate all exploiters, and so begins to 'wither away'.

Marx was a revolutionary because he thought the capitalist state would tyrannise the workers and use force to prevent them forming a democratic state. Force was therefore needed to resist this tyranny and create a democracy. Was this an undemocratic minority act? Marx polemicised strongly against the putschist ideas of people like Blanqui and he, Lenin, and Trotsky reasoned that one cannot found a state based on the mass of the people unless the mass of the people take part in its creation.

Benn's view of revolution as a minority act – guerilla war or an 'industrial coup' – was not theirs. Indeed they put their ideas to a more democratic test than parliament: they sought the support of a majority of the population. What government in Britain has had this? Thatcher took power with the votes of around twenty per cent of the population. What was this but an *electoral* coup? Why should our exploiters resort to a *military* coup when we tolerate such a thing? How have the ideals of socialism sunk so low that they call this 'democracy'?

Benn himself does not rule out the need for mass rebellion against a tyrannical state in all circumstances. He celebrates Tom Paine and the English revolutionaries, and agrees that if parliament were overthrown by force, then force would be needed to re-establish democracy. How does he differ from Marx?

It has been argued both by Benn and others that the critical distinction lies in the attitude one takes to parliament. But this idea, shared on the far left as well as the Labour Party's right wing, needs to be dissected with care. Benn's own distinction is between 'law breaking in pursuit of conscience' and 'revolutionary action to replace parliament'. Others have argued that revolutionary socialism is distinguished by rejecting the idea of a representative assembly, or denying the relevance of elections and the vote.[2] But the issue between revolutionaries and reformists in the last century was not whether they were for or against parliament and was certainly not about votes: it was their attitude to the *state on which parliament rested*.

British socialism has nothing to fear from elections if it has secured a democratic foundation for them: a lay, accountable, working class state. With this, it would get a majority in any representative body. True, our existing parliament could do with the removal of some ceremonial relics, and an elected second chamber might be an idea – perhaps made up of national and oppressed groups like the bolsheviks' second chamber.

Our present problem, however, is a different one. What should we do when parliament refuses to set up a democratic state? Should we wait for a parliamentary mandate for change, or press our demands regardless? Should we make it a condition of pressing ahead to victory, that we must have a parliamentary majority first?

Here, in my view, lies the true difference between Benn's position and the revolutionary socialist tradition in Britain. He argues that we *should* wait, if there is a danger of creating a new government that doesn't have a mandate from parliament. But parliament will not give a mandate to a government that threatens the state. And every democratic movement eventually threatens the state, which exists to defend the rich against the dispossessed. Benn is thus compelled to turn his back on the very movements he inspires, at the moment when they might fail to secure a parliamentary mandate and yet succeed by other means. Against Benn I lay the very charge he lays, in our interview, against the Bevanites: he lacks a strategy to *win*.

This, I believe, is why he did not resign from the 1976 Cabinet; this is why he now takes a firm and principled stand against the use of industrial muscle to oust Thatcher; this is the logic behind the idea of a 'truce' within the Labour Party. These are logical, principled and consistent decisions and fully refute the idea that Benn has adopted a revolutionary standpoint.

Contradictions arise because movements for democracy take a revolutionary course whether we want it or no. The miners were compelled to take on the Heath government because the only other option was retreat. The February revolution in Russia was planned by no-one; the German revolution of 1918 was a semi-spontaneous insurrection; as was the Portuguese revolution of 1974. A revolution can be prepared but not arranged, and the preparation consists only in saying 'enough is enough'.

In this sense only Benn therefore foments revolution while opposing it: Tebbit is right as to the effect but wrong as to the intention. Nowadays it is seditious to remind people of their rights. But this is the problem: once a movement for democracy begins one may not stand like Canute and dictate terms to it. The choice facing us is not whether to have a revolution but whether to support it; not whether to make a revolution but what to make *of* it. The issue is whether one embraces it and directs one's efforts to a democratic socialist outcome, or opposes it and opens the door to a terrible defeat. The issue is whether one chooses to win or chooses to lose.

Why does Benn counsel waiting for a parliamentary mandate? There is, after all, a contradiction in the idea that to create democracy we have to wait for the permission of an undemocratic body.

The most important argument is that in spite of all weaknesses, parliament remains a representative body. This argument is indeed powerful. Parliament is, after all, elected by universal suffrage. The vote does express a judgement on what governments do. Unless they prolong their own existence they have to submit to this judgment. Anyone who turns their back on a parliamentary decision seems to be turning their back on the people.

But not all parliaments are representative institutions just because they are produced by a vote, even of universal suffrage. And when we look at the parliamentary democrats that Benn champions – the English Revolutionaries, Tom Paine, the Chartists – we find that they were not fighting simply for a parliament but for a *genuinely representative* parliament.

Any elected body is only as representative as the state and constitution on which it rests. In Poland there is a parliament: that is, a representative body elected every four years by universal adult suffrage, with authority and power of veto over the executive. Hitler's Germany never abolished parliament: it merely abolished all parties except the Nazi Party. Indeed the German parliament legislated fascism, and the socialists themselves voted for the first stage of this legislation which banned the Communists.

Our parliament is 'more democratic' than these parliaments because of the existence of a plurality of parties, constitutional rights to organise, the existence of independent trade unions, and so on. Michael Foot discusses this in his *Observer* pamphlet: he dismisses, for example, Mussolini's parliament as a 'pathetic parliament' i.e. not a real parliament. But when is a parliament not a pathetic parliament? Did the elections of 28 March 1982 create a true parliament in El Salvador?

Benn argues that a British parliament would cease to be democratic if it prolonged its existence in order to avoid an election. But the British parliament has done this twice this century – each time during a war. The 1945 consensus was produced by such a government, the Churchill coalition. So how do we say whether a given parliament is genuinely representative? Benn, and many others on the left of the Labour Party, have done a great deal of work to show how parliament's representative character is interfered with by the media, by Whitehall's obstruction, by secret treaties, by the lack of party democracy, and so on. But are these not all manifestations of one and the same thing – *that our parliament is based on a undemocratic state and a class society*? Is it not therefore the case that it will *never* be representative while the state is capitalist?

This is directly relevant to the issues facing Bennism today. First of all the very basis of all parliamentary elections is the constitution of the land, to which MPs must swear loyalty. But this defines what is a legitimate party and what is a legitimate member of parliament. Any and every state protects itself by denying enemies of the state access to its parliament, thereby imparting a clear bias to representation.

This is the exact function of the vitriol directed at Pat Wall, the *Militant*, Tariq Ali and Peter Tatchell. This is the purpose of the witch-hunt in the Labour Party. Is this not the very reason that Benn's own philosophy is being redefined as a heresy? And the lines now being drawn – sometimes with great clumsiness – are placed so that the Labour Party and trade union leaders may assist the state in keeping out of the parliamentary chamber anyone who threatens the state.

Nor is this an abstract issue for a distant future when the revolution takes place. It is present today, because of the way that legality is tied to property and the legitimate use of force: it defines what constitutes extra-parliamentary activity. An example is useful.

In February 1982 blue-uniformed thugs, commandeered by privateer Arthur Snipe and commanded by Manchester police chief James Anderton, ransacked the Laurence Scott Engineering factory which was under the protection of its workers, who had occupied it against redundancy. According to current definitions the occupation was an 'extra-parliamentary action' by workers against the legal owner and the police attack was a legal action under parliament's protection to defend Snipe's property. This was not altered by police chief James Anderton's subsequent refusal to submit himself to scrutiny by elected representatives on the basis that he was comparable to Daniel, or possibly Jesus Christ.

Now a socialist government would declare it illegal to sack workers. It would declare that the occupying workers were its legal agents and that their instructions should be obeyed by the erstwhile owner and the police, who are in any case not needed to protect factories that the workers are perfectly capable of protecting themselves. Under these conditions the raid would have been a gross threat to public order and wellbeing, and an act of banditry to which any public-spirited citizen would respond by helping the workers place Anderton in Broadmoor and Snipe in the Manchester Ship Canal.

However, in the absence of a parliamentary sanction, those

who advocate such a course run the risk of prosecution for criminal conspiracy to riot, assault on a police officer, and mugging. Such people would be liable to be locked up, thrown out of the Labour Party, and denied any possibility of ever becoming an MP.

Yet this is precisely the course of action needed for the workers to defend their right to work. A choice therefore arises: if one is not to put one's parliamentary influence at risk, one is obliged *now* to retreat from offering the necessary support to those fighting to defend their freedoms. Parliament therefore neatly filters out all those who advocate the very actions needed to defend freedom, and to say the least lowers the possibility of a parliamentary majority for serious constitutional change.

In Britain above all this process is intensified by the role of the trade union leadership and the relation between state and party. Parties which seek office are obliged to seek a bill of health from the state; the threat against any candidate who does not toe the line is that of being branded as a leper – a heretic. But it follows that a party whose principal aim is elected office exerts continual pressure on its rank and file to choose candidates acceptable to the state. Careerism and opportunism can march hand in hand, which is why left wing constituency activists are constantly struggling against right wing candidates, and why the incidence of cowardice and treachery is so high in Labour's ranks. Not for nothing do the Labour faithful intone an annual hymn against these sins. They are merely expressions of the original sin committed when the ILP took its first bite of the state apple.

This ideological pressure, moreover, is backed up by a real material pressure: that of the trade union block vote and its financial clout. The trade union bureaucracy, like the state bureaucracy, is also a professional guild with its own interests, and these are allied to the interests of the state by the very fact that the condition for the bureaucracy's existence is as a *legal bargaining force*. The ultimate bargains are struck in the corridors of power, within the framework which our union leaders have learned through fifty years of support for imperialism: defence of the British state at home and abroad. The crucial difference, of course, is that the union leaders *are* subject to democratic control, the best democracy that exists today in Britain.

Yet this democracy cannot be fully exercised unless the rank and file can confront real choices. It is a dormant democracy. The deputy leadership campaign showed the power of this democracy when awakened. This democracy is lulled to sleep, however, by the division of functions between the unions and the Labour Party: as long as one does not discuss politics in the unions, nor mass struggle in the Labour Party, the giant sleeps and our Jack-in-the-Beanstalk bureaucrats can roam around the Labour Castle.

By virtue of the very fact that the Labour Party has no *function* of involving itself in trade union struggle and mass action, of linking hands with its trade union brothers and sisters, it may not wake them up and join with them against the abuse of the block vote.

Therefore, it is precisely because the Labour Party dedicates itself only to elections and to representing the people in parliament, that it *cannot* represent the people in parliament. Instead, it represents the trade union leadership who control it. The Labour Party negates its own declared aim, the reason for its existence: to represent working people in the Commons. Again, this is what the witch-hunts are designed to preserve: this is why a 'truce' is a travesty of democracy.

Only an activist party, linked in struggle to the union rank and file, can truly represent working people in elections. This leads us to the problem of winning the next election. Where does the initiative lie to recall or overrule parliament?

There is no right of the people to call an election. There is only a duty of the government to submit itself for election, at a time of its choosing. The legal right of recall rests with the monarch in his or her capacity as head of state; the effective right rests with the Cabinet.

The right to overrule the government rests with the guardians of the constitution, who are not elected: the Lords, the judges, and the monarch. In practice, moreover, the owners of private capital, particularly money capital, can provoke a government crisis when they 'lose confidence'. A run on the banks is a sanction on the government.

This is not a small matter. The most *vital* government decisions, taken at moments of crisis, are always taken in such a way that the people may not intervene on their own behalf in the decision. This includes decisions such as going to war, which twice this century has led parliament to prolong itself to avoid election. A third such prolongation may be self-defeating but this brings little comfort. In both wars and in Britain's most serious economic crises – 1931 and 1976 – there was a realignment of parties and a change of government by means of a coalition or near-coalition; in each case the initiative for the change came from the state; in each case the electorate were denied the right to intervene.

Even if a Benn-led Labour Party were to win a majority in parliament, would this also not lead to a comparable crisis? Would we not see a call for a government of national salvation to avoid the crisis? Would not a convenient group of deserters be found on the Labour back and front benches to do something their electors *never* asked them to do, which is to join a new coalition? This is the role of the SDP.

What is involved here is the idea that a vote continues to carry authority when the circumstances that give rise to the vote have changed. The government that sent half the working people of Britain to their deaths between 1914 and 1918 was actually elected to give Home Rule to Ireland and implement Lloyd George's social reforms. The 1929 government was supposed to start building Fabian socialism, not cave in to the slump. Wilson and Callaghan were mandated to go forward to the eighties, not backward to the thirties. How can parliament claim to represent people in relation to policy choices which were never confronted when the vote took place?

The reality is that the power to recall or override parliament rests with the state, which claims to act on behalf of the people. But this *on its own* virtually converts the state into a chamber of government. It means the state can *rule out constitutional change not previously agreed within the state*: in short it guarantees the defence of the state against parliament. Furthermore this immediately reflects back onto the practical, day-to-day choices available to the electorate. When, for example, a sterling crisis erupts and factories begin closing, parliament is constitutionally unable to take practical measures which make inroads on property: for example, to organise trades unionists to take over the banks and factories. Such measures would provoke a constitutional crisis so that the state may restore 'order' by deposing or overruling the government. Knowing this, parliament does not do these things. But as a consequence the electors are never given the option of choosing practical measures that will resolve the crisis in favour of working people.

Indeed, we may popularise a practical revolutionary attitude to parliament by saying that we, the working people, demand the same rights in relation to our representative bodies that the ruling class now exercises through its state on our behalf. Benn rejects the 'overthrow' of parliament. But what we demand is the right of the people to recall and to overrule parliament, a right the state *now* possesses under the constitution. Is this not what accountability is all about? How can one have a representative body that cannot be recalled or overruled by those it represents?

Parliament is accountable, not to the people but to the state; the state is accountable to its bankers – and the bankers are the trustees of the owners of private wealth. It follows that when we vote, we do not vote on who will represent *us*, we vote on who will represent our rulers. This is a valuable democratic right, a great improvement on absolutism or totalitarianism: but it is not what the Chartists fought for.

The stifling of initiative in the endless wait for a parliamentary majority, only to produce yet another betrayal: this is *not* the democratic road to change.

Does the foregoing imply, as the syndicalists thought, that parliament is irrelevant and socialists should leave it alone? This is still a common attitude on the British far left (and Benn has made many accurate and telling criticisms of it). Yet this too bears thinking about.

Lenin once publicly reminded the Italian communist Bordiga that 'without revolutionary MPs there can be no revolution'. Through parliament, the national political pulpit, one has a unique chance to rally the forces for change. Through it, the minority of the population that at any given time is actually engaged in struggle may win the support of those that are not, provided the chance is not wasted in futile parliamentary manoeuvres.

It is argued that revolutionary struggle loses votes. The *opposite* is the case: only by intransigent support for extra-parliamentary struggle at all times may one win a majority for genuine change. Hesitancy is what loses votes.

The issue is complicated in Britain by the structure of the Labour Party because it is a coalition in and of itself. By lowering one's sights, as the Bevanites have done, one may win a cheap election majority: but then the problems *begin*. In 1929, it is true that voters swung to Labour after the defeat of the General Strike. But the true test of this result is what happened when MacDonald betrayed. Can Labour resist a new coalition threat? Only if it can create a body of MPs with sufficient resolution to press ahead with the mobilisation of trade union and popular action to impose working class will on parliament, as in 1974. This in turn depends on whether, at the base of the Labour Party and unions, the rank and file are dedicated to this end and organised around it.

The problem is this. An extraparliamentary strategy asks working people, as did Marx, to liberate *themselves*. It therefore asks people to make much larger sacrifices and take bigger risks. The test of the vote, therefore, is the number of voters willing to commit, not just their MP but also themselves.

It is hence no longer good enough to preach. Working people need to experience their own power, and place confidence in their leaders not to abuse that power. It is after all easy, from the comfort of Westminster or a university library, to spin convincing arguments. It is another to convince one's sisters and brothers, in daily danger of losing their livelihood, to sacrifice everything for an unknown future. This is the weakness of a utopian approach: socialism is not just the great potential of tomorrow writ small, but the hidden achievements of today writ large.

If, therefore, we go to the polls on policies that call for action, then there must be convincing evidence already on the table that this action will succeed. The hesitancy felt by many working people towards Benn is not necessarily a right wing attitude: it is an expression of an instinctive understanding of just how hard the fight will be if he gets in. If, therefore, one says 'vote today and struggle tomorrow', the evidence on the table will be evidence of failure and the vote will be lost.

The idea that socialist revolutionaries will lose votes should therefore be rejected, as should the idea that being involved with parliament will taint revolutionary purity: on the contrary, it is only if the revolutionary tradition takes root and organises within the Labour Party that a movement *can* be created which can defeat the Tories, win the election, *and* defeat parliamentary manoeuvres, to force the implementation of socialist policies.

So can Britain's revolutionary tradition and its other socialist traditions coexist, and what should their relation be?

The further Bennism advances against the old Labour Party tradition, the more likely are working class victories. Yet Bennism itself contains the seeds of its own future failure. Britain's revolutionary tradition offers, in my view, the best hope for its working people and the best hope for the construction of a genuine workers' party, a genuinely democratic party – a revolutionary party. But the construction of such a party cannot bypass what is now happening inside the Labour Party, any more than the Labour Party can afford to ignore the revolutionary tradition in socialism.

In Labour's early days, all socialist traditions coexisted in its ranks. It was seen as a federation with genuine autonomy for all within it. The revolutionary British Socialist Party took part in its founding. The Communist Party, which grew from a fusion of the BSP with other revolutionary groups, sought affiliation to the Labour Party, took part in its activities and had two of its candidates adopted by local Labour Parties, who were returned to parliament as Communist Labour MPs, such as Saklatvala, MP for Battersea South in the 1924 government.

The majority of the Labour Party rank and file then believed the revolutionaries had a place beside them and welcomed their contribution. It was the labour leadership who introduced bans and proscriptions. Has the Labour Party been weaker or poorer as a result? These bans not only cut the party off from the Communists but from the hundreds of thousands of workers who looked to them. It created a situation within the party where every subsequent opposition that adopted ideas with revolutionary implications – as did every opposition that took democracy seriously – faced the agonising choice between breaking from the party ranks or bowing to the party leadership. It forced the ILP and Cripps' followers into the political wilderness at the time when it was most vital for their ideas to be fought for within the Labour Party; it forced the Bevanite group to bend the knee in the 1950s under the threat of expulsion for forming a 'party within a party'; and it will be used to try and extract a similar capitulation from the Bennites.

Eventually, I have no doubt, the present leadership of the unions are prepared to see the Labour Party destroyed rather than risk seeing it won, democratically and fairly, to positions that will seriously challenge capital in Britain. Eventually, I am equally convinced, the struggle for democracy in Britain must find itself compelled to undertake such a challenge.

The conditions for success in this challenge, and the conditions for failure on the part of those who oppose it, are that the Labour Party comes to terms with the hidden tradition of Britain's past – its revolutionary tradition. Today's revolutionaries themselves will be able to combine their forces with Labour Party members to achieve this aim if they, in recognising the nature of the convulsion that is overcoming both Britain and the Labour Party, come to terms with the issue which Tony Benn has placed back on the map in British politics – democracy.

Interview with Tony Benn

What led to your decision to stand for the deputy leadership?

You have to go back a bit. In '71, when I was chairman of the party, I made party democracy the main theme. After the defeat of the 1970 government, it became clear to me that unless you improve the democracy of the party, you were always likely to get into the sort of situation we had at the end of that government. Then, later that year, 75 Labour MPs took us into the Common Market by voting against a three-line whip and giving Heath his majority. That started the whole reselection campaign. The question of the election of the leader came up, because the PLP was clearly tending to get out of step with the views of the party as a whole. Finally the Callaghan veto on the '79 manifesto, on the symbolic question of the House of Lords, brought that issue forward. So you have to see the whole campaign against the background of the pressure for democratic reform.

In early 1979 I decided that whether Labour won or lost the election, I would not continue as before. If we lost, I wouldn't stand for the Shadow Cabinet, in order to devote myself entirely to the question of party democracy for a period. If we had won the election I would not have accepted office. I'm not even sure that I would have been offered office. I think that if Callaghan had won an overall majority, he wouldn't have offered me a job. But I wouldn't have accepted if he had.

I had a very long and difficult discussion with him in March 1979. He didn't know what I've told you, but he said to me, in effect, that he was not satisfied with the way I was operating within the Cabinet. That resolved me that I would then decide to devote myself to party matters if we won the election.

I then spent eighteen months on the back benches, and launched into the campaign on party democracy, as well as trying to put socialism back on the agenda.

Then Michael Foot became leader, by which time we had a theoretical commitment to an electoral college, although there was no specific arrangement. There was a lot of speculation then as to whether the deputy leadership should be contested when Denis Healey stood. The *Tribune* group decided that it would be more sensible not to have an election. I shared this view because I didn't regard the November 1980 election as having any legitimacy, following the earlier conference decision that there would be a new system. We wanted Michael to carry on in his capacity as acting leader, which he would have been able to do since he was the deputy when Jim went. But that view didn't prevail. I decided to stand for the Shadow Cabinet, really to show willing, wasn't elected, and later got co-opted, when Bill Rodgers resigned.

Now over that period, from the resignation of Callaghan until my decision was announced, there were continuous discussions as to what would be the right thing to do. I supported Foot as leader, and therefore there was no question of standing against him, but I discussed the deputy leadership with a lot of trade union leaders, and on a weekly basis with a group of people. My local party discussed it twice, and in February passed a resolution, on a motion from the chairman of APEX in South West, that I should stand.

I didn't want it to be argued that my candidature had in some way triggered off the defections, which it was quite clear were going to take place. But we wanted to do it early enough to have a political campaign at the trade union conferences through the summer, because it wasn't really about who won, but about the presentation of a total alternative to what was being argued by the then deputy leader.

This explains the timing: we held the announcement until 2 April. The statement that was published that day had gone round for consultation and went into about six drafts. I say this to show that the campaign was conceived as a political campaign, and it wasn't a decision taken in the middle of the night. The campaign was directed to the party, about the main policy questions and about party democracy.

And when did Michael Foot become aware that you were standing?

Well, while I was in the Shadow Cabinet I went to see him a couple of times, between the decision of my GMC in February and the announcement in April. He knew perfectly well, and I always played it straight. He strongly urged me not to, but I said in response that I understood his views, but had never known the leader of the party ever intervene in elections for deputy leader. It's never been the practice of party leaders to comment at all on elections, either to the Shadow Cabinet or to the deputy leadership, or to intervene in elections about their successors. Callaghan never said a word when Foot stood for election as deputy leader, nor a year ago when he succeeded him.

Where did your support tend to come from?

There were many members of the *Tribune* group, with whom I had worked over a long period. There was my local party, whom I take very seriously and who had given me very clear guidance on a whole range of matters including whether I should resign from the Cabinet in 1975 and in 1977. There was a lot of understanding and support from trade union leaders. The trade union movement, of course – particularly the left – have a great loyalty to the decisions of their own conferences. And therefore until their conferences had spoken, there was a certain shyness about speaking up. There's no doubt that there was support, and that this expressed itself throughout the summer, in that many of the sympathetic trade union leaders played a part in bringing about the 2.3 million votes that were achieved in the college itself.

Do you think that you will be placed in a position where you may stand for the leadership?

Well, my position has always been very clear. There was a vacancy in 1976 and I stood. And if there's a vacancy again I'm obviously a possible candidate. I've never been embarrassed by being asked that question. In '71 I think I stood for the deputy leadership when Roy Jenkins was already deputy leader, and in '81 I stood for the deputy leadership under a new franchise when Healey was already deputy leader. And I think that elections are a good thing. They involve discussion and debate, and renewal and political education. I don't accept for a moment that the 1981 campaign was in any way damaging to the party. I think it was wholly beneficial.

I think it was fortunate, in a way, that the mechanism was tested when we were not actually choosing a prime minister. It meant we could afford a few defects, but everybody who participated in it now knows very well that there will come a time when there is a vacant seat for the leadership, and when the vote will be determining who the leader – and hence the prime minister – will be. I think the experience of that six months will be extremely valuable for that purpose.

This would apply if there was a vacancy. However, many people feel that Michael Foot was elected to the leadership, essentially on the basis of representing the traditions of the left within the party, and that he's broken with that tradition. Do you think that there is a case for the left putting up a candidate in the near future against him?

Well, that's a different question. And just as the decision was taken collectively in 1980, so would any future one. I think what would influence people would be what was happening in the party. If there were a pressure to wind up the electoral college; to change its composition; to get away from recorded votes (which is one of the things which has caused greatest opposition from the right); and to reverse the policies on Europe, nuclear weapons, and the alternative economic strategy; then there is now of course the reserve way of appealing comprehensively to conference, namely by a candidature. I'm not saying any of that will happen, but that is why the party decided that it wanted to have an opportunity of putting a whole package together and saying we'll consider it.

But I think that, having said all that, I must also add that having spent two and a half years helping to get good policies – though with certain defects and gaps – we should now concentrate on getting out to people and not giving the impression, which would be wholly false, that what's going on is a bitter personal struggle for power within the party.

We've got to use this as the basis for campaigning vigorously and openly outwards on behalf of the people of the country who are in the middle of the most appalling and accelerating crisis. And I think that must be the dominant consideration in 1982.

Michael Foot expressly promised, at the Tribune *rally at the Brighton conference, that there would be no witchhunts. What do you think led to the change of position since, and do you think that there will be an attempt to follow this up by reversing the gains that you've just been talking about?*

Let me first say that I hope the main emphasis of the party's activities is outwards, supporting the unions against Tebbit, supporting local authorities against Heseltine, supporting the welfare state when it's to be run down, defending the unemployed, working for peace, and so on. I think that must be the main thrust of our action, and that will involve, of course, a lot of extra-parliamentary campaigning.

Having said that, there is bound to be an agenda and a debate at the annual conference. This falls, really, into three. One is: how do you attack the government's policies, and how do you organise? There, the difference will be between those who see it purely in terms of what I could call 'Commons-parliamentary tactics', and those who see it in terms of the mobilisation of the movement to explain what's happening and to defend our people.

The second argument will be the argument about policy, with an attempt to get the present very clear commitments watered down – on Europe, defence, and the economy. That would be between the 'Solidarity' campaign, put crudely, with the left on the other side. The third thing that will come up at conference will undoubtedly be attempts to change the composition of the college, its timing, and recorded voting. And the fourth thing which will come up, which is clearly going to be decided at conference, will be the composition of the executive for 1982-83. It seems to me that unless you carry the argument that we should only fight the Tories to ludicrous limits, there is bound to be an internal reflection of that debate within the party. That is what conference is about. So I think the process will continue.

It's certainly arguable that the process will be clearer, more precisely argued, if it isn't combined with what the press will be able to present as a struggle for power, in the context of where we are now.

If you ask about Michael Foot's position, you'll have to interview him. But he has reiterated that he is opposed to a witch-hunt, and his argument about the enquiry into *Militant* is that it's a very discreet and narrow enquiry to be undertaken by the general secretary, the national agent and regional organisers, to bring to light certain aspects of *Militant's* activities.

Militant are not a significant body in the influence they've had on policy. They are a body of people, the overwhelming majority of whose leaders have been in the party for many years, who got totally disillusioned in the Wilson years and restated socialism in a way that I regard as rather simplistic, and sectarian in character. But the real target of the right of the party is not *Militant*, which is just a convenient cover, but the whole new wave of people – of whom Tatchell is much more representative, as it so happens – who've come into the party, and whose main offence is that they are serious. It isn't that they're particularly left, or extreme, or dangerous or revolutionary or subversive, or that they're infiltrators; but they've come into the party to use it for its historic purpose of advancing the interests of the British working class movement. And that does of itself challenge the old parliamentary elitism, which has been a cover for the reversal of socialism as a result of three successive revisionist leaders: Gaitskell, Wilson and Callaghan.

I personally don't think that these recent advances are

reversible. Not least because there is now a party – the SDP – that embodies in its being, its thinking, its leadership, its philosophy, its record and its future, everything that the right wing of the Labour Party has wanted. The SDP is really what the right wing of the Labour Party wanted us to be. Having failed to achieve it, they formed a new party that does embody all this. The existence of the SDP makes it less likely that the Labour Party would agree to become a second class SDP. So I'm very confident, but of course the debate is going to go on vigorously.

Callaghan, for example, has been quite clear about what he wants. He is prepared to sacrifice the election to defeat the left. And perhaps he's not so unhappy about that, because it's a way of getting a coalition with the SDP.

Oh yes, there's no question about that. The Lib-Lab pact in '77 was the beginning of the Lib-SDP alliance. It was its forerunner. It's an amazing story, really, which has never been properly documented. The instructions that we were given after the Lib-Lab pact, to us as ministers, were that no business was to come to Cabinet committees until it had been cleared with the Liberal spokesmen. I literally had to see Penhaligon, who was the energy spokesman, before I could bring matters to the Cabinet.

Now, I'm in favour of a *Lab*-Lab pact. The Labour government should work with the Labour Party. But never in my career as a minister had I been told that legislation shouldn't come to a Labour Cabinet before being cleared with the *Labour* Party! If I had discussed it with the NEC before I brought it to the Cabinet, that would have been taken as an act of gross disloyalty, contrary to Cabinet collective responsibility.

But this might be a way the SDP could strengthen the right, instead of weakening it. When you say that the gains of the last period are irreversible, presumably you refer to, for example, the attempt to stop constituencies selecting the candidate of their choice.

Oh yes, but I don't think it can really be done. What has really interested me about the Tatchell case is the way support has spread across what I call the left-centre and even the democratic right of the party. They always use the language the other way round, but I think there is a democratic right, that has right wing views but believes the constituencies should have the right to choose.

Were we to get to the point where the NEC were able to determine who was and wasn't acceptable, then you really would be creating circumstances where the Labour Party would start to resemble, in its structure, the very East European states that the left is supposed to want.

But surely the right wing isn't simply going to give up this offensive. They will carry it even to the point of losing an election because they want to go in with the SDP. So doesn't it depend on whether the left organises to resist?

Well, I think the changes are irreversible in the sense that the constituencies, faced with a challenge of this kind, would continue to affirm their support for their candidates, and would go to the point where they were prepared to see the disbandment of their local party, rather than abandon their right to choose a candidate.

We all live in the shadow of our own history. Bristol East, before the war, had a member in Stafford Cripps. He was expelled in the '38 conference, on the motion of George Brown, and since the local party would not accept this, they were disbanded and a rump party set up. There wasn't an election, of course, until 1945, but when they tried to admit Cripps, he said, 'I'll only come back if you readmit the Bristol East Labour Party'. So they admitted the local party and Cripps at the same time.

I can't believe the unions would have their block vote used to create circumstances in which there were substantial disbandments, in which local parties said 'we are not prepared to support the candidate imposed upon us.' And with the SDP there, as an option for people of that view, it seems to me that the likelihood the Labour Party can be shifted off its

If they succeed, – and you can't rule out anything – then parliament would be a place where gentlemanly discussions took place about the marginal differences of emphasis between Roy Jenkins, Geoffrey Rippon, Ted Heath and Jim Prior, David Steel and Jim Callaghan, while the *real* argument in the nation took place outside parliament. You would be going back to before 1832.

The argument about what is called parliamentary democracy is now being presented in terms of Edmund Burke. It has nothing whatever to do with parliamentary democracy as the Chartists revitalised it.

But that is why history is so important, and also why we shouldn't be too pessimistic. Because from a very poor start, against the 1688 settlement and the 18th century Burke arguments, we managed to convert the whole thing into something that was a plausible imitation of what a parliamentary democracy *could* be like if there was a strong Labour and trade union movement operating. The fact that we've done it once means we must be able to do it again, but obviously the first problem is to ensure that we don't have to do it again.

You seem to be very optimistic that the Labour movement can resist. But the trade union leaders, at least, may well be persuaded that the left wing of the party will never be allowed to form a government. No matter how much sympathy you have for their policies, it will be argued, you have to recognise they will provoke the establishment into a panic. So we offer you a soft option – an SDP coalition. At least you don't have Thatcher on your back, and you can get a few reforms through. This may have influence on union leaders, and even lead to a strengthening of the right wing in the block vote.

You have to make a real assessment about this. The price that would be paid for adopting such a stand would be as follows. Firstly, you couldn't confine yourself to simply getting rid of the left or Tatchell, if you could achieve it. You would have to reverse the policies. There would be a danger that if you retain the pretence that you are going to get out of Europe, and so on, and it's quite clear that you're not, then you introduce such a massive incredibility into the whole posture of the Labour Party that in fact no-one will vote for it.

My own candid opinion would be that we would lose the next election disastrously if we tried to go on with the Labour Party as a two-headed monster. I don't want to imply that anybody doesn't want to win the next election. But the one thing that is clear is this: the dominant reason the Labour Party is doing badly now is that if you go canvassing, or speak at meetings, people say 'what is going to happen if we vote Labour?'. And if the public really thought that (a) we didn't believe our policy, that we wouldn't campaign for it and (b) anyway there is a secret intent to go in with the SDP, then they wouldn't vote Labour at all. They might just as well vote for the real SDP instead of a fake one. So this would be a recipe for defeat.

There's a very good passage from Clem Attlee, where he said that the essence of MacDonaldism was fascism: the belief that there was some national interest and that this overrides party factiousness. He finishes up by saying 'It was the steadfastness of the rank and file of the labour movement which saved British democracy'. And I don't think that's an exaggerated presentation.

I think all these arguments are very powerful. What worries me is the extent to which they will be accepted by the union leaders.

You imply that there's a difference between them and their rank and file, but if you take the trade unions, then just consider what's going to happen in the next six months. You're going to have this massive Tebbit onslaught. You've got local government being destroyed. You've got the welfare state being destroyed. Events are going to radicalise the Labour Party, and when it actually comes down to it, is it really the case that at the Labour conference 1982, delegations are going to say, 'our prime objective must be to destroy the influence of that very part of the Labour Party, namely the Labour left, that is giving the most vigorous support to us in our struggles'? I don't think it's going to happen.

Of course, whether the unions respond to this attack by going left or right will depend on how they succeed in resisting these attacks. Because, as you said, if people are frightened, then they tend to move to the right . . . (Benn: In the short run) . . . *In the short run. But therefore, one could say that the fate of the next two conferences is in some sense bound up with the successes of the trade unions in resisting the Tories. And of course the big industrial upsurge of 1974 turned the tide in favour of left wing policies. So presumably this would mean that, for the Labour Party left to be successful, it would have to continue supporting trade union struggles, which is rather a break with the kind of tradition of, let's say,* Tribune.

This is where the deputy leadership campaign played such a part. There was an identity of interest between the constituencies and the unions. I'm not implying this was anything to do with who the candidates were, but for one period, and for the first time ever, there was *one* issue which was political in character, which was being discussed in every CLP and every trade union conference, relating to policies.

It did something else too. It tested the internal democracy of the unions in a way that was quite interesting. Tom Jackson wrote to Ron Hayward and protested that I'd gone to Brighton to speak at a meeting, when his conference was in session, as if there was a five mile limit. Now the effect of that in stimulating the broad left in the UCW was formidable. And if you look round the broad lefts, they're now developing very rapidly.

I think there's another way of looking at it. If the industrial strength of the unions has been to some extent undermined by unemployment, it's going to drive the trade union movement to political action just as, after the general strike, when there was a setback in '26, the trade union movement went in a political direction. That's very desirable. But you can't, having been defeated or weakened on the industrial front, then turn to *right*-wing political policies. You're going to turn to left-wing policies, radical policies.

Well, how true is that? Let's take 1926 as an example. I agree that a tremendous left-wing sentiment grew up. But after 1926, wasn't it rather the sentiment of a minority? And in fact a coalition government was inflicted without a great deal of resistance, and followed by a long period of Tory or National rule?

Well, I don't know. The history of the twenties in my mind suggests that there was a big surge of industrial action which led to disaster. And three years later Labour was the biggest single party. Then in 1931, MacDonald betrayed. If you read the minutes of the 1931 Cabinet what is so interesting is that the NEC capitulated but the TUC general council was absolutely resolute. Admittedly the Cabinet leadership betrayed, but – and here's the difference – the betrayal within the Labour leadership this time is a betrayal that's already been siphoned off to the SDP three years before the election.

So, I don't want to sound foolishly optimistic, but I think it's very important not to wring your hands and say, 'All we can do is riot in the streets and everything will be all right'. I'm not saying you're suggesting this – but my own opinion is that if the Labour Party simply united around its own constitution, as amended, and its policies, and campaigned for them vigorously, there would be an enormous restoration of confidence in us.

This leads onto another question, on which it seems, your views have changed: to what extent the left in the party should organise. For a long time you stood above the organised groupings like Tribune*, and so on. Now you've joined* Tribune *and you're helping set up a new grouping, the Labour Liaison Committee. Do you think this represents a change in your views, or has the situation changed?*

That's very difficult. I was asked to join the Bevanites by Fenner Brockway on behalf of Nye Bevan in 1951. But I felt then, and still feel now, that it is important that the left isn't marginalised within the party. Also I didn't want to subject myself to the discipline of a party within the party. And I stuck to that position for a very long period, for a variety of reasons.

In the end I joined the *Tribune* group early in 1981 after a great deal of heartsearching, because I felt that it was an opportunity to be present once a week in a place where there was discussion going on. Having said that, the *Tribune* group does suffer from two difficulties. One is that it is a closed meeting. Secondly, it has been rather meticulous in not maintaining a continuing link with the movement outside. Now there's a group of members who meet every day in the House called the 'Campaign group.' The Campaign group bases itself on the very opposite principles. First of all, it is open to any MP who wants to come along. Secondly it has absolutely open door to anyone who wants to look in. It's like a collective surgery – one day it might be some students from a polytechnic who come, another it might be someone in an industrial struggle, telling us what's happening, so that we can respond immediately. And I do think that that is necessary.

But I think it would be a mistake for the left to marginalise itself within the Labour Party by having what was an organised left that tried to be centralised, and separate. I think that the best way of doing it is to see it in Liaison terms. There are a mass of organisations – the LCC, IWC, CLPD and so on, the broad lefts, and what we really need is a chance to keep in contact with one another, without trying to impose a standard ideological position.

It needs to be ad hoc in character, year by year in organisation, and working for the clear objectives of an effective fight against the government, a defence of our policies, and defence of our constitutional changes, and some perfectly proper and legitimate role in trying to see that conference gives us an NEC that will be supportive of these things.

Now, that is the way in which I think it will shape up. We've a meeting in January, at which it's going to be discussed, and I don't think that marginalises, nor does it reproduce the *Tribune* group.

So, essentially the outstanding features of this new grouping are that it is open, it bridges parliamentary and non-parliamentary sections of the movement, and it doesn't draw a particularly rigid ideological division but bases itself on the policies of the last few years?

Yes. A programmatic co-operation on an annual basis. Very loose in character, outward looking in its main thrust. It would be inward-looking only insofar as we had to deal with matters in the party to sustain and permit an outward-looking campaign directed at the public at large. Now, it is an experiment like everything else. But I think about the right formula, and it's been very fully discussed, and I think will be seen to be necessary. After all the recent attacks on the left will have created the demand for the very thing which it will meet.

It is interesting to contrast this 'new left' and the old Tribunite left. You said, and I agree, that one of the most important differences is the idea that the Labour Party must involve itself in campaigning activity such as support for trade union struggles – which, as you say, have never really been an aspect of Tribune. *Beyond this, certain sorts of views in the party seem to go together: for example, if you believe that it is possible to go on working within the 1945 consensus, that the main sphere of party work should be within parliament, and that trade union action should be separated from political action, and if you are against devolution, then you incline towards the views of the old Tribunite left. The new left seems to be rejecting the idea that the 1945 consensus can be maintained, or is calling for a radical shift in the balance of power and wealth and thus wants constitutional changes. Perhaps this reflects quite deep forces inside the Labour Party.*

You mustn't intellectualise it into too fundamental a division. Because as a matter of fact if a Labour government was elected tomorrow that did just what the 1945 government did, it would be so revolutionary that it would take your breath away, because things have deteriorated so rapidly. So in a way the so-called radical left, and so on, has lowered its sights back to 1945, while rejecting the consensus politics that flowed from '45. So you mustn't discredit the 1945 initiative.

Oh, I'm not at this point questioning the 1945 programme. The point here is the difference in reaction to the fact that the programme is no longer acceptable to capitalism. What seems to have emerged is that the problem of British politics is that even the attempt to implement 1945-type policies produces such convulsions. If you like, there are two reactions to the fact that the old methods don't produce the old results. One reaction is to say we have to change the objectives, and the other is to say we have to change the methods.

Absolutely. It's an indication of the decline of the system that moderate demands for jobs and homes and schools require such radical policies, so that the demands are moderate, but in order to get them you do have to mobilise outside the group of forces that in the first place brought the Labour Party into existence as an effective force.

This time round you have to recognise that you couldn't just catch capitalism in one of its good years and manage it to your advantage. You've got to make the changes and then recognise that there would be structural and ownership and democratic changes that would have to be built in to sustain it, so that it couldn't be taken away a second time. And I think that is the difference. And that, of course, is what frightens the establishment. They are producing a great fog of confusion, which they hope will buy enough time for capitalism to recover and then marginalise labour for ever and ever. But objectively it can't be done.

Now, I think there is one other difference about the role of the left. Clem Attlee used to speak of the left as having a 'minority mind'. It was a very bureaucratic way of describing it. They really wanted to be in opposition, he said. And then he said, you know, you must be ready to take responsibility. And it followed in his argument that you then came to terms with reality and you didn't argue the left case.

Now, that criticism was a very stinging one. But I think that it is true to say of the 'old left' – whatever that may mean, and I don't want it to be identified with individuals – that in a sense they didn't have the will to win. They were content with being allowed to make the case, to lose, to be patted on the head for being good losers, and then to take a place in a Labour coalition which didn't do it.

Then, of course, they were free to say 'we really would have liked to have gone further'. But that's not good enough. You've actually got to want to win. I don't mean for individuals. I'm talking about the fact that you've actually got to want to do it. And it is the determination to win the argument, and press it, and do it, that characterises the new left. It's serious. It's not engaged in a sort of game that safeguards their consciences, and allows everybody to say 'well, you did your best pal, you've made your point, thanks for helping'.

I think there's a vitality on the left now, whereas the right wing in British politics generally, and in the Labour Party, is bankrupt. It hasn't got anything to offer. And that is why it is turning to all these scapegoat solutions to its problems.

So: vitality, confidence and seriousness, against emptiness, scapegoatism and cynicism is the difference between the two.

Perhaps we could now turn to the roots of your own thinking. It seems to me that your christianity plays an important role. For example, you use the bible as a source of authority. Do you feel there is a conflict between this and the christianity of most organised churches and religions?

I see myself as a student of the teachings of Jesus, and the mystery and theology of it doesn't excite me as does the social message. If you look back at history, there was an injection of the very radical idea of human brotherhood, which had a huge revolutionary potential, and was suppressed for that reason over a long period.

I have absolutely no association with organised religion, and I think there is no more connection between the teachings of Jesus and organised religion than there is necessarily between socialism and organised socialist parties. Having said that, you've also got to admit that, for example, the marxist catholic priests in Latin America are very courageous people.

They are fighting the same sort of battle which was fought by many of the dissenting Christians who allied themselves with the Labour movement in the early days, and you have to take that into account.

We must not deny ourselves access to a meaningful interpretation of our history since for many centuries religious debate was the vehicle in which political ideas were carried.

Finally I think you've also got to take into account that there is a moral dimension, which cannot be excluded by Marxism. For example, one of the most powerful arguments about Tatchell, whatever you say about the merits of the case, is that here is a person who was punished and not heard. Now that raises questions of natural justice, and you can't exclude it. It is also true to say that the values of capitalism, which entirely disregard human values, have never been able to obliterate the idea that you had an obligation to your fellow men and women.

So, for all these reasons, I believe that religion is a very important part of our history and tradition that we blank out and exorcise at our peril. But you mustn't think of me as a pious or devout person who is in some way trying to keep alive church traditions that have been overturned by history.

The moral aspect of any movement of social revolt is very powerful. Apart from anything else it is the factor of unity and legitimacy for the movement. In fact, there is an interesting parallel, because when religion was the main source of political authority, practically every movement of revolt was also a heresy.

Oh, yes. Do you know about Pelagius? Pelagius was the only real British heretic. The church devoted centuries to eliminating his ideas. In effect he subscribed to justification by works and not faith: saying that people, by behaving decently to one another, could enter grace without necessarily believing.

This was a total threat to the church of Rome. Pelagius was a characteristic British heretic. He had all those pragmatic and moral qualities which drive doctrinaire establishments up the wall with anger, and this is a deep part of our history and absolutely unconquerable. I have a facsimile of the only remaining copy of John Tyndale's bible, for example. It was illegal to read the bible until 1549. Why was it for the first 1500 years of the christian faith in Britain illegal to read the bible? It was because it encouraged people to think all sorts of dangerous thoughts!

I do find, and this is exactly what makes it so interesting, that all these arguments have gone on for centuries, and if people don't understand it because of anti-religious propaganda or because the church is so reactionary, this has the unfortunate by-product of blanking off all the reading we should be doing to understand how it was presented before, and how gains were made before.

You have also referred to Marxism's positive contribution to socialism. What influence has Marx actually had on you?

I'm ashamed in answering this question, at my own intellectual ignorance. I was brought up in a socialist home where socialism was discussed, so I had a perfectly impeccable background where commitment was concerned. But I studied at university, which was supposed to provide a great course on modern civilisation, but where Marx was only referred to very casually and dismissed as having no relevance and having been wrong on the labour theory of value.

Now, as the years have gone by, a number of things have interested me. First of all, the extent to which, a hundred years after his death, Marx's name is still used as a term of abuse, rather than as a key to interpretation. I'm giving the Marx memorial lecture in February, and I'm writing and preparing for that now. In the British Museum I asked them to check how many books there were about Marxism, as opposed to Freud, Darwin and Einstein. There were over a thousand on Marx, a hundred on Darwin, 300 on Freud and I think 200 on Einstein. This intellectual domination by Marx is unknown to the British people. It seems to me essential to preserve the legitimacy of the Marxist contribution to British socialism.

Secondly, when you read the Communist Manifesto, and see the staggering foresight of those who, in 1848, saw with precision what is happening now, you feel as if this is darkest England where these ideas cannot yet even be contemplated. Actually Britain has given birth to the three main economic and political philosophies: those of Smith, Owen, and Marx.

Finally, of course, the distortion of the Marxist idea that developed in Russia was as great, and of the same character, as the distortion of the Christian teaching at the time of the Inquisition. But it is as wholly wrong to blame Marx for what was done in his name, as it is to blame Jesus for what was done in his.

Robert Jenkins in his book begins by identifying me as a Christian dissenter, and ends up by saying I'm a voluntarist Marxist. Well, I'm a student of Jesus and a student of Marx, trying to make the best use of the analytical weapons available.

You have referred a lot to the British tradition. But when you talk about Britain you seem to mean English; in the list of those who have inspired socialist thought in Britain you seem to omit Scottish and Welsh thinkers or James Connolly. Also, to what extent is the British tradition really British? Tom Paine spent a long time in France and America, and this wasn't regarded as exceptional or unusual by the Chartists either, who were strongly influenced by the ideals of the French and American revolutions. Have we stepped back to a rather insular view of socialism, and should we not try less to celebrate the peculiar Britishness of our tradition, and look more at international influences?

I accept what you say, but let me explain why I've done it this way. First I have reflected the excitement of my own late learning of socialist history. I didn't know much about the Levellers, but when I was asked to do the Burford lecture in 1976 I spent six months reading about it, and came out with the fresh enthusiasm of somebody who had discovered a great bit of our tradition.

I discover old things, and try to put them together. The media not only blank out half or more of our own present voice, but with the help of our historians they blank out our history. Now, if people don't understand that what they are doing is in line with what their grandparents and ancestors did, they think 'this must be foreign and strange. Why should we try something here that has failed in Russia, or failed in Poland, or whatever?' It is important that people should be as comfortable with their political ancestry as they are with their family story.

Britain has influenced other countries: we had the first European revolution, and we have a proper place in world history. But of course the international traditions have to be upheld, and this is one of the reasons I want Marxism to be put back on our agenda. There has got to be an international market place of ideas, in order to understand the international world we live in.

So it is in that sense, not in a nationalist sense, that I do it.

You seem to be saying that the British tradition is uniquely peaceful. We have a parliamentary tradition. But is that necessarily a peaceable one?

I don't think any history is necessarily a history of peace. The history is of struggle, and the struggle sometimes becomes violent.

Some people speak of parliamentary democracy as if we've had it since 1295. In point of fact we've only had universal suffrage this century, and one woman, one man, one vote at the age of eighteen since 1970. And by then we'd already lost many of our sovereign powers that parliament could exercise on our behalf. The role of the people, vis-a-vis whatever stage of primitive parliamentary government we had, was a role of demanding. As the landscape darkens and we swing to the right, I see the historic role of the labour movement and its paid officials – for that is what an MP is – as formulating our demands. The whole managerial tradition, which has grown up while Labour was the natural party of government, has been absolutely destructive of that role.

We are really the representatives of an economically disenfranchised people, demanding at the gates of power the right to jobs, to homes, to schools, dignity, retirement, peace, social justice and so on. And that is an extra-parliamentary role.

There would be a Labour Party if we didn't have a single MP in parliament and there would be a function for us.

If PR succeeds in cutting or strangulating the umbilical cord, between parliament and public, then parliament will become increasingly irrelevant, and the external struggle will become more important. And then external pressures will force even that sort of a government to respond.

As to the question of violence, I have never had any doubt whatsoever that if no democratic route to peaceful change exists then there would be a moral right to revolt in any country. That was laid down in the American Declaration of Independence. And that right to revolt is an inherent right, vested in the people themselves.

Having said that, the way in which the debate between extra-parliamentary violence versus parliamentarianism has developed on the left is, I think, highly diversionary. The way it has been presented is that 'you'll never change things by using the parliamentary mechanisms'. Therefore by the use of force – normally a general strike – you would succeed in seizing power, and then when you got there, in some way it is alleged you would be better placed than if you had got there by consent.

Now I see two defects in that. Firstly, if I believed that, which I don't, I would be busy digging out my old manuals about how to use a Lee Enfield, drilling, and working out how to get into the BBC studios on the day of the revolution. This would be a total diversion.

Secondly, if you did get to power that way, you would not have public support behind you, and when the crunch came – and the crunch would come for a socialist government that came to power by a coup, just as much as a government that came to power by consent – you would not have the public with you. You would be easily overturned, because the subversion of international finance will be brought to bear with even more zest, with even more public support for it in this country, if you come to power illegally.

So I think this is diversionary, a part of the pessimism of the ultra-left, or what ever you call it – and in fact makes it the agent of the right. Because the final victory of the right over the working class would be to persuade them that whatever they did, they couldn't win.

Now, of course, the Tories have never had these arguments. They know perfectly well that their real power lies outside parliament. It always has done. It lies in the City, with the landowners, administration, or the officers, or whatever. They see their job as getting into parliament by persuasion and then using their time there to give public assets back to their friends and attack the working class. Generally speaking, this is the civilised and legitimised class war. It was once said that the Tories don't talk about the class war because they are too busy practising it.

We can go into these tremendous theoretical arguments about how many angels can stand on the head of a pin – but it is a strange discussion, because the reality is that if we can mobilise support, and press for things, we can get them even from Tory governments.

The problem is that many British working class people are not yet aware of their condition, and don't understand what's happening because the media prevents them from doing so. They don't organise together but remain divided between black and white, men and women, and so on. Our task is to help the people to understand, not only the nature of their condition but the need, the necessity, the relevance of socialism, and organise themselves in such a way as to use their majority to see that it comes about. And it *can be done*. My criticism of those who call themselves revolutionaries is that they speak as if reform had been tried and had failed. Reform hasn't been tried, and I think the revolutionaries are really revolutionists, left-talking revolutionists. I don't think there are any real revolutionaries in Britain. There may be dreamers, but there is nobody on the left who is actually planning and preparing themselves on the assumption that the transfer of power will come by revolution.

The debate between reform and revolution in Britain has been posed by many on both sides as if the choice were that you either use parliament and renounce force, or prepare for an insurrection and boycott parliament. It seems to me that quite apart from whether it is correct or not, this has not applied in history. Indeed, people seem to have been most violent in defence of democratic rights, and in our history, parliamentary rights.

Historically, the debate seems to be about how far you are prepared to go in struggling for popular sovereignty. The most left wing component of any movement for social change has generally been a movement which, by one means or another, has insisted on popular sovereignty above all else. To this end it has carried the struggle against all unaccountable *sources of power through to their conclusion.*

Yes, of course in theory the trouble is – and this is why the right wing has a certain credibility – that those who lead movements for popular sovereignty, having won campaigns in the interests of popular sovereignty, then set up a dictatorship of the proletariat and become antidemocratic.

Yes, that's the classical argument.

And I think that it is a perfectly proper anxiety to have. But of course Mugabe had a long civil war, which was the most violent extra-parliamentary activity, or violent revolution, and was satisfied by a victory that offered one person one vote.

Exactly. So I would like to explore a number of situations where the conflict between parliament and movements of social revolt has been put to the test. First, where there is an attempt by violence to unseat a democratically elected government, you have said that it would be legitimate and indeed necessary to defend that government by arming the people – for example in Chile. And if a Labour government were so attacked, we would have to defend it by, if you like, unconstitutional means.

Well, here you come to an important issue. I agree with the general proposition that the defence of democracy must entitle you to resort to arms. It's the same argument as if you were fighting a war. If a foreign invader were taking over your country, you defend your own democracy and way of life by resisting militarily, and that would apply internally as well.

We have a very peculiar constitution, where the ultimate reserve powers have been preserved for the establishment. I've written about this in *Arguments for Democracy*.

If a coup in any way found favour in the eyes of the establishment, they could use the constitution to blank out democracy. That problem is the unfinished business of 1688. You could be in the position where Lord Denning might find the law required him to blank out the democratic processes in the interests of the constitution of this country.

Sure. But let's now take Hitler's rise to power. He didn't come in through a coup. He was elected. What took place was that the strength of the labour movement, which was the only real defence of democratic rights, was dissolved in effect by dissolution of the parties and unions. And the excuse was an alleged terrorist attack on the Reichstag.

If this were to happen here – erosion of democratic rights to the point where parliamentary democracy was no longer democratic, but simply parliamentary, then presumably it would be necessary to defend democracy by other means than through parliament.

Well, I've written about this too. We were having an argument over the Industrial Relations Act, and Callaghan was saying 'obey the law, obey the law'. I argued two things in response to that. One of which was that if, by perfectly democratic parliamentary means, the Prime Minister – then Heath, now Thatcher – were to prolong parliament, then she would break the social contract in Rousseau's sense and the moral legitimacy of the government would go. If the government were, for example, to re-introduce the Combination Acts, and all trade unionists were carted off to jail, would we sit back and say that this was the law and it must be obeyed? Clearly you have various ways of dealing with that. One is by saying that you have inherent rights which cannot be removed. Secondly we all have the right of conscience against the law. This is another way of playing the moral card, and that sounds very cynical. But by taking a moral position, you then force the establishment to go to the point where they lose public support.

If they then lose public support, power will come back to you in terms of electoral victory. But if they remove the democratic electoral mechanism, then the right of revolt exists.

However, I think that this is to some extent a theoretical discussion – but still a very meaningful one – because while the powers of the ballot box remain, and while the rights of the unions remain, then I think that the likelihood of that happening is slight. You don't want to spend too long working out what would be the Dad's Army defence of democracy, in a society where it's not likely to be challenged.

The reason this could be relevant is that if there is an attack, of a fundamental kind, on democratic rights here, then it is unlikely to take the form of a coup. There would be such tremendous resistance to a coup that it's very dangerous for the establishment. But many would argue that it would take the form of a steady erosion of the effectiveness of parliament for use by the Labour Party, to the point where it is impossible to exercise sovereignty through parliament – if it ever was.

Well, I think that is already beginning to happen. That is why I wrote about Britain as a colony, and said that in significant areas of policy, parliament has been conned into abandoning the responsibilities entrusted to it by the people.

So successful was trade unionism and the ballot box in putting the working class in a position where they could transform society democratically, that at that moment a treacherous establishment handed over the keys of the kingdom to people who would see that it never happened. This has already begun to happen, and at least we've got to air these problems now so that people realise. And actually they did begin to realise, to an astonishing extent before we did that the parliamentary process was not able to exercise all real power.

Then, to that extent, it's not just a theoretical possibility we've been talking about (Benn: No, it's the real thing.) *It's the real thing, so if we have the right of the people to revolt against tyranny, and we are living under a disguised tyranny, then do we not have the right to rebel?*

I think the problem about that arises if you really do decide to nail your colours to the mast of democratic renewal. This is what I believe in. I believe democracy is the most revolutionary force of all; that we've never really had it in full and that to the extent to which we had it, it is being taken away. What we are now witnessing is the emergence of a Democratic Renewal Movement. Not in the old liberal-capitalist sense but in a very broad industrial, economic and political sense.

Now, you absolutely *destroy* your chance of being heard on that score, if you're saying that democracy has got to be renewed by revolution or violence. Because then people say 'Ah! That's what it's about! The assault on democracy is from the revolutionaries!'. Actually, what I'm saying is that it's a democratic renewal movement against counter-revolutionaries, who are trying to take away our rights.

The language we use has to be precise, because people are entitled to know what we are saying. If they think we are trying to organise a coup against what they're told is democratic, instead of trying to achieve a democratic renewal of what is not democratic, then the people, quite rightly, would not support us.

This problem applies, though, to the legitimacy of any act of rebellion, not necessarily a revolt. Simple defiance, for example, of the government and its laws, is defiance of parliament too, and – it is argued – the will of the electors. The question of legitimacy is here very important too.

Well, it would be an inherent legitimacy. There are certain inherent rights which we are entitled to assert. And quite manifestly, parliament has no moral right to take away our inherent rights. And that is why the argument must be conducted at the moral plane, as well as on the economic plane.

Let's take Islington. I've been reflecting on Islington and parliamentary democracy. The people of Islington voted in a Labour council and three Labour MPs. They have now, by defections, been denied the choice of the party that they've chosen to represent them, both locally and nationally. What does an Islington citizen, who believes in parliamentary democracy do? There has been a coup in Islington. People put in under one colour change their colour, and purport to represent and indeed are the loudest ones prattling about parliamentary democracy.

How does the Labour Party respond to that? Does the Islington party go to the leadership and say: 'we believe in parliamentary democracy and we've been denied our rights'? What will the Labour Party say? Well, suppose they say, 'whatever you do you mustn't engage in extra-parliamentary struggle'. So OK, you vote for three more MPs – but they may defect. How many defections must there be before the people of Islington say, 'well, we've tried your method, and quite frankly it hasn't worked, because we're never allowed to have our own representative'?

But then if the Labour Party in Islington had known this was going to happen two years ago, and had said 'we're going to recruit members to get rid of these people, who we don't trust', they would have been told that they were undermining parliamentary democracy which is what is said of Tatchell.

So there are lots of areas in which extra-parliamentary and parliamentary struggle have to be conducted simultaneously. I do think our liberties are being taken away, and I believe that if the SDP were elected they would take them away even more actively. But the trouble with the word revolution is that it is inextricably associated with violence, and extra-parliamentary is associated with anti-parliamentary, and you're in danger of throwing the baby out with the bathwater. We ought to be saying: 'we are a reforming, democratic movement. We believe in inherent rights, the right to organise, the right to vote, the right when voting to get a commanding position on behalf of the majority of the electorate, and the right to use that commanding position to resolve the grievances that lead us to discontent'.

From our own tradition, the question is whether we do have at our disposal a democratic instrument capable of being used, or whether we don't. Now, I think we do have. And I think we marginalise and minoritise ourselves by pretending that the potential for democratic change doesn't exist.

And I believe that the assertion that democracy through parliament, or parliamentary democracy, *can* be effective, is a very important assertion to make. And I also believe that the revolutionists who I agree with you are not really revolutionaries, are diverting people's attention from what could be done if only you could get a majority to do it.

Well, they're diverting people from what can be achieved by extra-parliamentary action too, by denying the connection between the two. But let's take one more case, quite like Islington, which is what has happened to the GLC. Here entrenched prerogative, which was never sanctioned by the sovereignty of the people, is being used to deny the right of the electorate. But in that case, doesn't a similar sort of situation apply as in the case of the Pentonville dockers? Do people have the right to defy the law?

Well, Lord Denning is the real opponent of parliamentary democracy. He believes that an appointed judge has or should have an inherent right to rule as unconstitutional an act of parliament. Now he is saying that the GLC has gone against an act of parliament. But that isn't the only fact that should be taken into account. Because he himself believes as he said in his Dimbleby lecture that even if the act of parliament *did* allow the GLC to do it, he should be entitled as a judge to rule it out on the grounds of public policy, which he is best qualified to assess.

So some of the judiciary, very foolishly in my judgement, have now identified themselves quite explicitly with what many marxists and socialists have said about them, namely that they are enemies of democracy. And if I were a practising lawyer or judge, I would be deeply worried by what Denning and the House of Lords have done.

As to the Pentonville Five the TUC did respond. It said that if they weren't released by Monday there would be a general strike. I was then chairman of the NEC, and we unanimously passed, on my motion, a resolution that we would support a general strike if they weren't released. So don't think that when it comes to the crunch even the TUC and the NEC, which wasn't 'leftwing dominated' then by any manner of means, was not prepared to take action.

Well, that's very much the kind of thing I mean. I hope Michael Foot isn't proposing to investigate this. But if we accept the extra-parliamentary defence of, and the legitimacy of, democratic rights, then the problem that now arises is as follows: there is very often no dividing line, either in people's minds or in what they do, between placing demands on a government, and, at the point where it refuses to concede them, trying to depose the government in order to replace it by one more favourably disposed. In Poland, for example, the leaders of what began as a reform movement clearly concluded, at a certain point, that they could achieve their ends only by actually taking the law into their own hands and trying to replace the government.

That is a very good example, isn't it? You had in Poland a socialist government that came to power by a coup. They installed themselves in the interests of the dictatorship of the proletariat, and then governed without consent. Then they met resistance, which got out of hand because there is no mechanism for dismissing the Polish government. That did lead to a revolution and a military counter-revolution, immediately. They are back, now, with a government, under martial law, which has no mechanism for seeking or winning public support. That is the very difference between Poland and here. If the situation here gets to the point where the People's March for Jobs, or the Jobs Express, led to riots and a direct clash, the government's support would plummet and we could get a change of government by the ballot box.

It's very important not to underestimate the power of the ballot box. The establishment don't. They think there's too much democracy in Britain. We would be very foolish if we gave away the one asset that has got public support, that is on our side, namely the democratic route to change, and said 'well, because it's reached a certain point, we're going to try and topple you'. Because I think that would actually produce a counter-revolution. It would lead to a coup taking place before the election even occurred. And then the people engaged in the coup would be saying, 'we're doing it in defence of democracy', which is exactly the argument that we accept, quite rightly, if our own democratic rights, of an elected government, are taken away by a coup.

But is Britain in reality so different? In the following sense. Firstly, we have many, many obstacles to parliament actually being sovereign . . .

Well, parliament isn't sovereign, it's the people who are sovereign. We have to distinguish that.

Yes, but a constitution which places powers outside their hands; a law which is used to defend a privileged minority; a police force which is clearly biased against the working class, black people, women; property laws that disenfranchise workers from control over the economy; and so on. Could this not produce movements of revolt which would feel quite justified, in the first instance, in going to parliament and asking it to do certain things. And on finding it doesn't, trying to intervene more and more forcefully – I would say forcefully, rather than violently – into parliamentary life. This is, after all, the process which unleashed the English Civil War. It began by people gathering around parliament, attempting to influence, and then – it was said – intimidate members of parliament. They were in fact accused of assembling 'Mobs' outside parliament.

Well, I suppose that's what they are trying to accuse Tatchell of advocating.

Of course, and this is the reason why, for example, there is a law which says one cannot hold demonstrations or assemblies within a mile of Westminster. Now I wonder whether a really deeprooted and determined movement – made up precisely of people who are serious, confident, and all the rest – would in fact stop and say 'Let's wait until the ballot'.

This would depend on whether they felt they had confidence in their representatives in parliament, however few in number, to be articulating their case and doing something about it. I think that a lot of the frustration that people feel is that they think whoever they vote for, they're going to end up with the same sort of government.

But you're jumping several stages in this process. If there was injustice, a sense of outrage, expressing itself in demonstrations, a feeling that nobody in there was going to support you, and that even if you won an election you weren't going to be allowed to do it anyway, then you would have circumstances in which, out of hopelessness and despair, people would take the law into their own hands. If, however, the mechanism which we have fashioned so carefully over the years is working, and the discontent accurately reflected, and people feel that what they are saying is being said with them and for them, and on their behalf, and that there is a party there that has the relevant remedies, that would meet their need, and that an election is coming, and if they win the election remedies will be found, then I think democracy is safe.

But what you are predicating is a situation in which all hope is blanked out, and therefore people would turn to violence. Now, if they did turn to this remedy, an awful lot of things would happen. First of all, because it was an act of war against the democratic machinery of government, a lot of people would be frightened, and you would get an immediate counter-revolution which would blank out their rights even more. The repression would be even tighter.

Secondly, people who tried it would be disillusioned because it would fail, and they would sink into even deeper apathy and acceptance. So I think there is a danger in exploring (though intellectually it's important and we should think it out) as if it were the primary question, the full nature of the potential betrayals, to the point where people say 'well, why wait, we'll do it tomorrow'. We have got to put hope back into the democratic system. Frightened people will turn to the right, and that applies if they're frightened to the point of sporadic and disorganised violence – because that's what it would be. It wouldn't be organised revolutionary activity, but sporadic acts of violence which would be repressed.

Why should that be the case?

Because I think the scenario you've just set out would lead to people saying 'well, to hell with it! We'll just burn the place down, we'll burn down the BBC – for example'.

Well, can we take a more practical example: the Lib-Lab pact. Wouldn't there have been some justification in the TUC saying 'this government, and what this government has been doing, has been imposed on us by methods that have nothing to do with democracy, over which we have no control. It is not legitimate, it does not express the sovereignty of the people. So we're going to call a general strike, and the demand of this general strike will be that people who express the policy of the Labour Party should form a majority in the Cabinet'. After all, is this any different from what the bankers do, except that it is in favour of democracy? Does it seem unrealistic or impossible? Wouldn't people have more hope and confidence if they thought the TUC could be relied on to defend democracy in this way?

You've got to consider very carefully what you're doing if you argue that. There are other ways of doing it. I think the disengagement of the TUC from direct involvement with the government, which I believe the TGWU executive is talking about in relation to the NEDC, and might certainly apply to trade union members of public corporations, would be very effective. Because it would remove the veneer of legitimacy from government/union relations, in circumstances where you feel that the Rousseau-type social contract has been broken.

There is a very good case for the withdrawal of the Labour peers from the Lords, saying, 'we are no longer prepared to accept that this place has legitimacy'. And I think the GLC judgement might be the occasion for this even though the Lords was acting in its judicial capacity.

Then we should look at ending pairing in the Commons, where we would say that we don't want to be part of a cosy mechanism for planning government business, when the government business involves the withdrawal of our basic democratic rights. More directly, you could, for example, say 'you'll have a majority of 300 on your bill tonight, because all our members are out in their constituencies talking to people whose rights have been taken away'. And so on.

I think that methods of that kind, which are direct in character, but not undemocratic in the way they can be presented, offer a way of revealing the nature of what is actually happening. But the line I draw, and it is a very important line to draw, is this: a country that has the right to 'destroy' a government by the ballot box should not be diverted from the task of executing that absolutely unique and historic right. The one really important thing about our democratic process in Britain, and it's absolutely fundamental, is that it *is* a synthetic revolution. It *is* the destructive power of the general election that matters. It *is* the fact that you can get rid of, sack, remove, rusticate, dispose of a government without bloodshed that is the most important right we have.

Indeed, that is why proportional representation is so dangerous, because it actually negatives that power to 'destroy'. All you would then be able to do would be to have the christmas pudding coalition mix stirred time and again but with no power to dismiss the whole government. And *that* is the danger of PR that people are not *really* aware of. Now, all this talk which we've had, which I find very interesting, is a diversion from the fact that we have within our grasp the power to remove the Tories within two years from now. And the sooner we get on with it, the less we waste time discussing the circumstances in which the power workers could cut off the electricity to the House of Commons if Tebbit's bill removed trade union rights, the less we think of that the better. But of course in saying that, we've got to be clear that our power rests outside parliament just as Tory power rests on the class base of ownership of capital.

You see, most people in the world would give their eye teeth to have the rights we have won. To say that because democracy is abused, because rights are taken away temporarily, that all is lost, would really be to abandon a democratic power which has enormous potential. That potential is understood by our opponents, even though we don't appear to understand it ourselves.

What you are saying is, despite all the erosions of democracy which have taken place, that we do still have this right to change governments through elections?

We do, and our failure to be the sort of party that is able to do it, our recognition that we've failed to prepare ourselves to exercise that historic role in the discharge of that responsibility through the ballot box, is the reason we've been so inward looking, because the fault lies in ourselves. And until we can clarify our own position, we'll never be able to get people to see, or believe us in our analysis, our campaigns, and our remedies.

But Mugabe himself would never have had a civil war if he'd had even the imperfect democracy we now have. The Americans would never have had to have a revolution, the Levellers and Cromwell would never have gone to war, if at any of the stages in history you draw parallels with, there had been this supremely well-oiled, well-tested, well-trusted mechanism that we have here, with all its defects. The winter palace would never have been stormed if in 1917 the Russians had had the rights we have. The Poles wouldn't be engaged in conflict, if they had the rights we have. So, it's absolutely proper to talk about these matters, but what we must do is keep it in proportion, and above all within the framework of our own achievements – which give us every reason to think that if we *can* do it, we *can* offer hope, we *can* change things. And that is what we should now set about doing.

References

Place of publication is London (or in the case of Penguin Books, Harmondsworth) unless otherwise indicated.

The following abbreviations are used throughout.

AfD	Tony Benn, *Arguments for Democracy*, edited by Chris Mullin, Nottingham: Spokesman Books 1981.
AfS	Tony Benn, *Arguments for Socialism*, edited by Chris Mullin, Penguin 1978.
Biography	R. Jenkins, *Tony Benn: A Political Biography*, Writers and Readers 1980.
GGL	Tony Benn, *The Role of the Trade Unions*, Granada Guildhall Lectures, Granada 1980.
Speeches	*Speeches by Tony Benn*, edited by Joan Bodington, Nottingham: Spokesman Books 1974.
WE	*State Intervention in Industry: A Workers' Enquiry into the Labour Government*, Coventry, Liverpool, Newcastle and North Tyneside Trades Councils 1980.
WWW	*What Went Wrong*, M. Barratt-Brown et al, Spokesman 1976.

Prologue, pages 11-15
1. *GGL*, p.47.

1. The Enemy Without pages 17-30
1. *Biography*, p.99.
2. *Speeches*, p.44.
3. Andrew Glyn and John Harrison, *The British Economic Disaster*, Pluto 1979, pp.52-3.
4. *Biography*, p.126.
5. *Biography*, p.89.
6. *Biography*, p.75.
7. *Biography*, p.76.
8. *Biography*, p.81.
9. *Speeches*, p.201.
10. *Biography*, p.223.

11. *The Times* 7 December 1973.
12. *Annual Abstract of Statistics* 1951, 1966, 1976, HMSO.
13. *Speeches*, p.94.
14. *Biography*, p.131.
15. *Biography*, p.127.
16. *Biography*, p.128.
17. *Speeches*, p.79.

2. The New Politics pages 31-58

1. *Speeches*, p.226.
2. *Speeches*, p.228.
3. *Biography*, p.151.
4. *ibid.*
5. *Speeches*, p.114.
6. *Speeches*, p.255.
7. *Speeches*, p.35.
8. *Speeches*, p.164.
9. *Speeches*, p.38.
10. *Speeches*, p.36.
11. *Speeches*, p.164.
12. E. Bernstein, *Cromwell and Communism*, Nottingham: Spokesman 1980, p.54.
13. *Speeches*, p.164.
14. *GGL*, p.45.
15. *Speeches*, p.37.
16. *Speeches*, p.26.
17. *Speeches*, p.20.
18. *Speeches*, p.164.
19. *Speeches*, p.289.
20. *AfS*, p.154.
21. *The Listener* 21 May 1981, pp.665-666.
22. *Speeches*, p.11.
23. *Speeches*, p.31.
24. *Speeches*, p.19.
25. *AfS*, p.72.
26. *AfS*, p.43.
27. P. Kahn and A. Scargill, *The Myth of Workers' Control*, University of Leeds and University of Nottingham 1980, p.3.
28. I. Roxborough, P. O'Brien, J. Rodick, *Chile: the State and Revolution*, Macmillan 1977, p.89.

3. The Enemy Within pages 59-80

1. *WWW*.
2. P. Addison, *The Road to 1945*, Quartet 1977.
3. *Speeches*, p.76.

4. *AfS*, p.48.
5. *WE*, p.37.
6. *AfS*, p.125, footnote. See also AfD, p.184., where Wilson is quoted confirming this incident.
7. *AfD*, p.11.
8. *WE*, p.37.
9. *AfS*, p.126.
10. *AfD*, p.18.
11. Tom Forester, 'Neutralising the industrial strategy', *WWW*, p.90.
12. *WE*, p.114.
13. *WE*, p.35.
14. *WE*, p.36.
15. H. Wilson, *The Final Term: Labour Government 1974-76*, Michael Joseph 1979.
16. *WE*, p.34.
17. Tom Forester in *WWW*, p.85.
18. *WE*, p.44.
19. Discussion with author, December 1981.
20. Ken Coates, 'Whatever happened to industrial democracy?', *WWW*, p.126.
21. *AfS*, p.64.
22. P. Kahn and A. Scargill, *The Myth of Workers' Control*, University of Leeds and University of Nottingham 1980, p.9.
23. Dave Bailey, 'The Enigma of Workers' Control', in *International*, Vol. 5 No. 1.
24. *Biography*, p.229.
25. *Biography*, p.229.
26. Discussion with author, December 1981.
27. *Biography*, p.247.

4. Rethinking Socialism pages 81-108
1. *AfS*, p.145.
2. *GGL*, p.39.
3. *WE*, p.44.
4. Hain (ed.) *The Crisis and Future of the Left: the Debate of the Decade*, Pluto 1980, p.47.
5. *AfS*, p.139.
6. *AfS*, p.146.
7. *British Business* 27 March 1981, p.613 gives detailed investment figures broken down by sector for each year of the Wilson-Callaghan government.
8. London CSE and the Labour Co-ordinating Committee, *The Alternative Economic Strategy*, CSE Books 1980.
9. *The Balance of Payments* 1981, (The Pink Book), HMSO.
10. *AfS*, p.164.

11. *AfD*, p.6.
12. *AfD*, p.11.
13. *AfD*, p.9.
14. Speeches, p.107.
15. *AfD*, p.13.
16. *AfD*, p.196.
17. *AfS*, p.163.
18. *WE*, p.34.
19. G. A. Phillips and R. T. Maddock, *The Growth of the British Economy 1918-1968*, George Allen and Unwin, 1973, p.139.
20. D. Thompson, *England in the Twentieth Century*, Penguin 1965, p.103.

5. From Benn to Bennism pages 109-135
1. S. Rowbotham, L. Segal, and H. Wainwright, *Beyond the Fragments*, Merlin 1980.
2. *GGL*, p.47.
3. *AfD*, p.172.
4. *AfD*, p.194.
5. *Listener* 21 May 1981
6. *Speeches*, p.283.
7. *AfD*, p.18.
8. *AfD*, p.190.
9. Tony Benn, 'Is Britain a colony?', *New Socialist*, September/October 1981, p.13.
10. Michael Foot, *Observer*, 17 January 1982.
11. *AfD*, p.189.
12. R. Crossman, introduction to W. Bagehot, *The English Constitution*, Fontana 1963, pp.39-42.
13. *ibid*.
14. See, for example, D. Kogan and M. Kogan, *The Battle for the Labour Party*, Fontana 1981.
15. Michael Foot, *Observer*, 17 January 1982.
16. *Tribune* 17 January 1982.
17. Discussion with author, December 1981.

Epilogue pages 136-151
1. K. Marx, *Critique of Hegel's Philosophy of Right*, Cambridge: CUP 1970. See also S. Avineri, *The Social and Political Thought of Karl Marx*, Cambridge: CUP 1968.